Building
High Performance Government
Through Lean Six Sigma

A Leader's Guide to Creating Speed,
Agility, and Efficiency

Mark Price

Walt Mores

Hundley M. Elliotte

New York   Chicago   San Francisco   Lisbon   London
Madrid   Mexico City   Milan   New Delhi   San Juan
Seoul   Singapore   Sydney   Toronto

1 2 3 4 5 6 7 8 9 0 DOC/DOC 1 6 5 4 3 2 1

ISBN: 978-0-07-176571-8
MHID: 0-07-176571-9

e-ISBN: 978-0-07-176607-4
e-MHID: 0-07-176607-3

This publication is designed to provide accurate and authoritative information in regard to the subject matter covered. It is sold with the understanding that neither the author nor the publisher is engaged in rendering legal, accounting, or other professional services. If legal advice or other expert assistance is required, the services of a competent professional person should be sought.

—From a Declaration of Principles jointly adopted by a Committee of the American Bar Association and a Committee of Publishers

McGraw-Hill books are available at special quantity discounts to use as premiums and sales promotions, or for use in corporate training programs.

This book is printed on acid-free paper.

Contents

Acknowledgments

This book is representative of the great work that our colleagues are providing to our many clients every day. In particular, we would like to recognize several of our colleagues who helped us make this book become a reality:

Matt Reilly . . . for his leadership and unwavering support of seeing this project through to completion

Larry Oglesby and **Mark George** . . . for their thought-provoking insights

Marc Tatarsky and **Paul Jaminet** . . . for helping navigate the waters of getting a book published

Throughout this book we have recognized ten contributors who helped develop the chapters in different Parts of the book. We want to thank this incredibly talented set of individuals for their unique insights and passion for delivering high performance to our clients.

We'd also like to thank **Greg Parson** and our friends at the Accenture Institute for Health and Public Service Value for their thought leadership and contributions to this book. We applaud their efforts to deliver better social, economic, and health outcomes for global citizens.

Special thanks go to **Laura Ikeda** for assisting us through every step of the way, and to **Sue Reynard** who patiently worked with all of us and pulled our thoughts together and helped turn them into coherent prose.

Finally we want to thank our families for their patience and understanding during the many nights and weekends required to complete this special project. So, thank you to our wives **Julie**, **Alex**, and **Amy**, and to our children **Emily**, **Alex**, **Eva**, **Jordan**, **Jake**, **Ben**, **Caleb**, and **Hundley, Jr.**

The Third Lever

Cutting services, increasing budgets, or raising taxes are not *your only options*

N o corner of government has been spared from turmoil in recent years. What has been the main challenge for your organization? Severe budget cuts? Increased demand for services? Unanticipated responsibilities? Calls for "improved performance"? More likely, some combination of these.

Demands for better service and improved responsiveness by government agencies and organizations have been on the rise for reasons that make the headlines every day: the fight against terrorism, national security issues, broad-scale natural disasters, public health scares, rising health care costs, and drastic shifts in business sectors and economics. At the same time that more is required of government, budget pressures have increased. Government organizations with small discretionary budgets have seen cuts or increased demands with no way to respond to them. Other organizations have witnessed dramatic shifts in priorities. And even those with a temporary boost from stimulus spending face long-term uncertainty.

Those of you trapped in the demand vs. resources squeeze are probably having one or both of the traditional options paraded before you: (1) ask for a budget increase so you can increase services and (2) cut services. You may be embroiled in handling conflicts over the outcomes demanded of your agency or department, the level and sources of the funding required to support your work, and how the dollars should be allocated across various programs.

Neither cutting services nor raising taxes is particularly palatable, but many public sector organizations are making these hard choices every day. When the state of New Jersey elected to live within its means and made significant spending cuts without raising taxes to meet an $11 billion budget gap in 2010, it faced some tough times: layoffs of 1,300 state workers, closings of state psychiatric institutions, an $820 million cut in aid to public schools, and nearly half a billion dollars less for aid to towns and cities. As a result, New Jersey saw the largest student protests and standoffs with teachers' unions it had seen in years.

What if there were a third option besides increasing budgets or cutting services—an additional lever you could pull to get more and better services while controlling costs? That lever exists. It's called **High Performance**: continually improving the **outcomes** you deliver to the public while simultaneously lowering the delivery cost and improving **cost-effectiveness**. Figure 1 shows how High Performance combines successful outcomes and cost-effectiveness.

Figure 1: Components of High Performance

Building High Performance Government Through Lean Six Sigma: A Leader's Guide to Creating Speed, Agility, and Efficiency will show you how to create the foundation for moving from wherever your organization is today to a higher level of performance. Our goal is to help you **deliver the outcomes you are required to deliver for 10–20% less than it costs you today, while maintaining or improving service for your customers.** Moving to the upper right quadrant of Figure 1 increases your organization's **Public Service Value** (PSV)[1]: how much benefit the public sees from its tax dollars and fees. PSV is the public sector equivalent of what is called "private sector value creation."

Is 20% too conservative a figure for potential savings?

The promise that you can reduce your costs 10% to 20% may sound high to skeptics reading this book. But we believe it is actually a conservative figure representing the cumulative impact of improvement efforts—and individual areas can expect much greater savings.

For example, Ohio Shared Services, which the Buckeye State set up in 2009 as the first statewide shared services center for back-office functions in the United States, could provide a model for more efficient and cost-effective government worldwide.

By processing a number of key financial tasks—accounts payable, invoice processing, travel expense reimbursements, and vendor maintenance and management—that were previously siloed among individual state agencies, Ohio Shared Services is reducing duplication, freeing agencies to focus on their core functions, and driving significant cost efficiencies.

The state has already realized 15% to 20% improvements in productivity, while its costs for processing travel and expense reports **have been cut by 67%**, from $37 to $12 per transaction.

In time, Ohio expects to achieve about $26 million in average annual savings, or about $500 million over 20 years.

Putting the Challenge in Context

The methodologies and practices behind High Performance are long-established in the private sector, as demonstrated by the success of companies such as Procter & Gamble (P&G), Apple, Colgate, and Intel. Some of these ideas and practices are gaining a foothold in the public sector.

In recent years, our colleagues at the Accenture Institute for Health and Public Service Value have studied dozens of public sector organizations around the world to identify the strategic and operational principles for creating public value. Combining their research with our long experience in helping private sector businesses create shareholder value and our more recent work in the public sector has led us to identify three essential ingredients for creating a High Performance public sector organization:

1. **Being outcome-focused and citizen-centric.** An organization can be considered high-performing **if it delivers the right outcomes and *only* the right outcomes** to the public. That means allocating your budget

to delivering programs that truly reflect the priorities of your customers, whether another government agency or citizens. Meeting this standard is a constant battle for many public administrators as they attempt to balance the needs of a diverse constituency. The "right outcomes" for a public urban transport system, for example, require a finely tuned portfolio of travel options that includes buses, trains, airports, light rail, highways, bike paths, and pedestrian sidewalks. The portfolio must also reflect the geography and preferences of the taxpayers who reside there so that it supports the economic, social, and cultural life of the city.

"Citizen-centricity" in action

Each year in France, 120,000 people initiate the naturalization process through the country's Home Office. Officials in France set out to address process delays and improve customer satisfaction with the process. They wanted a simpler process that was easier for applicants to use and also more consistent and fair across the 70 offices that handled naturalization requests.

Subsequent improvement projects were chosen based on their potential of contributing to those goals. The new optimized processes have achieved the goal of handling cases in less than six months. Efficiency and time-to-serve at implemented sites have improved by at least 20% and by as much as 32% (the rate varies depending on baseline measurements taken at the start of the project at each site). Improved workflows have reduced stress levels and increased consistency and applicant satisfaction.

2. **Focusing on the distinctive capabilities needed to deliver on the mission.** Every organization performs a wide range of tasks, some crucial to meeting short-term or long-term customer needs (the "distinct capabilities" required to deliver on the mission) and some needed simply to keep the organization running. High-performance government organizations are unshakeable in their efforts to develop specific capabilities that support the services or products they deliver and at the same time to minimize their effort in everything else (including the option to outsource non-distinctive work). For example, the U.S. Defense Logistics Agency (DLA), as its name implies, is responsible for getting equipment and supplies to the U.S. armed

forces wherever they are needed, anywhere in the world. The agency manages more than 4 million consumable items and processes more than 30 million transactions worldwide. The most important use of DLA resources would be building its expertise in "supply chain optimization" since that is its distinctive capability—the thing that is most critical to being able to successfully fulfill its mission.

3. **Building a Performance anatomy for your organization.** The term "anatomy" is used to represent the structure of an organization. A Performance anatomy gives an organization the elements it needs to deliver outcomes exceptionally well—with the highest quality and productivity levels—and to be responsive to shifts in the public's needs. A Performance anatomy for the National Institutes of Health, for example, would have to include the capabilities to rapidly and effectively review proposals and award grants and to provide for world-class oversight of diverse research projects. To construct a Performance anatomy, public sector leaders must be willing to adopt methodologies that will maximize targeted outcomes within their budget limitations.

In summary, to achieve the highest level of performance, government organizations must determine and clarify which outcomes they want to achieve, and what it is they *will do* and *will not do* to achieve those outcomes. Then, they have to deliver the most services possible for taxpayer dollars, and they have to do it with an effectiveness and efficiency that is on par with the best companies in the world.

What's in This Book

Knowing what outcomes your organization needs to focus on and the distinctive capabilities you will need to deliver those outcomes are important components of becoming a High Performance Government Organization (HPGO). But the true enabler of both those elements is the third component: **creating an organizational anatomy capable of delivering the outcomes and generating the distinctive capabilities you need at peak cost efficiency**. Building a Performance anatomy is the challenge we address in this book (see Figure 2, next page).

Figure 2: Performance Anatomy

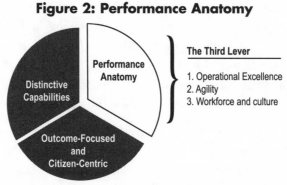

The nuts and bolts of building an organizational design have been covered extensively in other resources. The purpose of this book is to provide overall direction and context to help public sector leaders answer the top-level questions: Why does high performance matter? Are the rewards worth the effort? Where should we start? What will have the biggest impact on my organization's ability to achieve more? How can we innovate cost-effectively? How can we be more responsive to the changing needs of taxpayers? How do we make our operation more effective and more agile? How do we create a performance-oriented organization?

Meeting the Challenge

There's a lot of talk in the public sector about the **New Normal**: a condition where budgets will never be as flush as they were in the past, where the old mantra "doing more with less" is replaced by a never-ending call to "improve productivity" or "do even more with even less." In the New Normal, change will be constant, and the ability to react quickly will be a survival skill.

Now is not the time to support government functions that have become slow or convoluted. Life in the New Normal requires our governments to operate more efficiently, solve real problems quickly, and become much more nimble. Given the U.S. federal government's operating budget of $2 trillion, implementing just 10% in efficiencies across government operations could save as much as $20 billion per year.

Building High Performance Government Through Lean Six Sigma was written to help government leaders get started down that path.

CHAPTER 1

Building the Anatomy for High Performance

Because of its ability to withstand attack by improvised explosive devices (IEDs, including homemade bombs), the mine-resistant, ambush-protected vehicle (MRAP) has become a critical asset in protecting our warfighters across the globe. Demand for MRAP vehicles increased virtually overnight, from about 200 vehicles for the U.S. Marine Corps in late 2006 to more than 15,000 vehicles for the combined services by early 2007. In response to growing public concern about the adequacy of U.S. warfighters' field resources and protection, the U.S. Congress mandated delivery to Iraq of 1,500 MRAP vehicles by December 31, 2007.

Achieving this mandate required a rapid acceleration in production from 10 vehicles per *month* to 50 vehicles per *day*. The Navy and Marines were faced with a seemingly impossible challenge: increase output by a factor of 150, as quickly as possible. Building more facilities was out of the question because it would take too long. Simply throwing more and more bodies at the problem wouldn't generate the results needed (at one point the final assembly plant did reach maximum staffing and operated 24/7 but still fell far short of the 50-vehicle-per-day goal).

The leaders of the effort realized they needed a new approach that would generate greater productivity *within* the resource and time constraints they faced. There were three main components to the path they followed:

- **Adopting practices for achieving *Operational Excellence*.** These included continuous process improvement (CPI) methods that eliminate waste and improved quality throughout a process (key to increasing productivity 150 times without requiring 150 times more resources). Most importantly, the leaders approached the challenge with an **enterprise view** of the production processes, meaning they looked at how to make all the pieces of the puzzle work together most effectively, end to end.

- **Driving a rapid response (*agility*).** The leadership committed its own workforces and budgets appropriately. Recognizing the congressionally mandated timeline, the leaders brought in outside experts who guided decision making and drove innovation while internal resources were being brought up to speed.

- **Shifting the *culture*.** This will create a learning environment in which workers were encouraged and supported in their efforts to obtain and apply new skills and tools for attaining Operational Excellence and agility.

Together, these three components—building Operational Excellence, developing agility, and creating a supportive culture and workforce—set the foundation for increasing output and quality while reducing the amount of resources and cost needed. These components give an organization the right **anatomy for achieving high performance**: the capability to continually improve productivity and to deliver more mission for the cost.

Targeted improvements in the MRAP assembly operation were launched in August 2007. Production had reached 10 vehicles per week by that time, thanks to a combination of increasing the number of workers (= higher budget) and some initial Operational Excellence improvements. Unfortunately, production was still far below the target.

Only by adding in the other two components of Performance anatomy—agility and culture—did MRAP production reach its 50-vehicle-per-day goal just four months later, in December 2007. (Published accounts cite 2008 production figures that occasionally rose even higher, to 70 vehicles per day.)

This book looks at the three components of a Performance anatomy from a leadership perspective, examining key leverage points in each area. To lay the foundation, here is a quick overview of each component.

Component 1: Operational Excellence

It is likely that you have heard the term Operational Excellence before, perhaps framed as the ultimate goal of adopting a particular continuous improvement methodology. Some related terms you may be familiar with are process improvement, Lean Six Sigma (LSS), Lean Transformation, and business reengineering.

We use the term Operational Excellence in its broadest sense to mean **maximizing outcomes for the cost**. That definition describes a comparison that is not yet widely recognized in the public sector: *that the value delivered by an organization will always be judged against the cost to deliver it.* Operational Excellence means you can continue to deliver more and more value for less and less cost.

The comparison between value and cost is important for every organization and is becoming increasingly important in the public sector. Managers and leaders are under constant pressure to decide where and how to best allocate shrinking or limited resources. In government organizations, the investment decisions are often complicated by regulatory requirements that mandate how portions of the funding must be allocated. This further pressures the organization to create favorable outcomes within prescribed funding limits.

More or better services does not have to mean higher cost

In the past, the mind-set of most organizations (whether public or private sector) has been that they would be happy to offer more or better services *if only they could get more budget.* Conversely, if their budgets are cut, they would be forced to cut the quality or quantity of services.

Use of Operational Excellence (OpEx) nullifies that equation. Organizations that have implemented OpEx methods have seen that they can drive costs down *without affecting service levels.*

The Ohio Shared Services group described in the prologue, for example, is able to provide all the administrative services formerly provided by separate (and redundant) functions while dropping costs as much as 67% in some areas (see p. 3). You'll find other examples throughout this book.

Key attributes of organizations that achieve Operational Excellence include:

- **They understand and communicate what is important.** They have a clear sense of mission, have identified their customers (the people and groups who use their services or products), and have expended the effort to deeply understand what those customers value most.

- **They are constantly evaluating their own performance.** They have identified metrics linked to strategic and operational goals and monitor the metrics regularly to evaluate progress and gaps.

- **They link improvement efforts to strategic priorities.** Improvement efforts at every level are linked to cascaded priorities; each effort drives the execution of agreed-upon strategic priorities.

Working toward Operational Excellence has many beneficial side effects. Think about the training that runners do to lower their time in a 5K race (a desired outcome). They need to make a number of "operational improvements": develop more efficient strides, control their breathing, and develop better running technique. As they make these improvements, they see additional benefits, such as better muscle tone, fat loss, decrease in resting heart rate, shorter recovery periods, and so on. Those benefits come along with achieving their key outcome, building speed for the 5K.

In the same way, High Performance government organizations gain from Operational Excellence in secondary ways. Besides the direct benefit of delivering on current outcomes with improved efficiency and effectiveness, they display execution excellence across other aspects of the enterprise (see Table A).

Table A: Benefits of Operational Excellence

	Effectiveness	**Efficiency**
Primary Benefits	Improved quality Improved speed	Improved process speed Decreased operating costs
Secondary Benefits	Increased customer satisfaction Enhanced customer-centricity Enhanced/improved features Reduced complexity Improved reliability Increased flexibility Improved sustainability	Improved productivity Increased throughput Improved process cycle efficiency Improved decision-making productivity Improved asset management Decreased risks/improved certainty of outcome

For example, suppose a public safety organization wants to reduce crime levels—an outcome. It conducts a survey to find out what citizens value most, which turns out to be a quick response when they report incidents. After identifying a range of possible actions that would contribute to faster responses (a citizen-oriented outcome), the organization makes operational improvements that consistently decrease response time. That effort leads to greater citizen satisfaction, a side benefit of a chain that started with a strategic focus on an important citizen-oriented outcome. This cascading of priorities is vital to the success of any organization as it plans investments and channels resources to achieve its desired outcomes.

Part I provides detail on shaping an effective Operational Excellence effort.

Component 2: Agility

For all the known challenges that public sector organizations face, there are many more that we can't anticipate. Two years before the Navy was required to start producing 50 MRAPs a day, few people, if any, recognized the need for a vehicle resistant to IEDs. Two weeks before the collapse of the banking industry, the U.S. secretary of the treasury had no idea that his office would soon be in charge of $700 billion in bank bailout funds.

Citizens are expecting higher performance and demanding more from government despite a relatively fixed investment. As the world grows more complex and intertwined, the pressure to be agile—to respond quickly to new and evolving demands and needs in innovative ways—grows every day. Challenges can occur without warning; yet we can be sure that something is likely to happen. Agility allows an organization to adapt, change, and innovate quickly.

In the past, agility in the public sector was largely associated with those few agencies or departments that respond to emergencies: the Federal Emergency Management Agency (FEMA), fire and police departments, rapid deployment units in the military, and others. But more and more, public sector leaders are seeing that the future will require *every* organization to be more agile than it is today, in one or both of these dimensions:

- **Short-term agility:** the ability to respond within days or weeks to a sudden change

- **Long-term agility:** the ability to anticipate and respond to longer-term changes

Public sector organizations that master both short-term and long-term agility will be sources of strength and national or regional competitive advantage for their populations. The highest-performing government organizations possess the ability to both respond rapidly in the short run and to look out over the far horizon and make changes before the next challenges reach them.

The U.S. Army is a great example of an organization that has mastered agility in equipping soldiers. After the deployments in Iraq and Afghanistan, Army soldiers and leaders quickly identified modifications and improvements to their equipping sets (the term used for the suites of assets required by a combat unit, including tanks, guns, spare parts, etc.). Rapid changes in battlefield conditions meant that they needed to be able to change the combination of assets in each equipping set with lightning speed.

However, traditional operations were more focused on the long term and not well suited to the rapidly changing short-term needs of soldiers in the battlefield. In quick response, the Army created the Rapid Equipping Force (REF) to work with soldiers and leaders in combat situations. A separate organization with its own funding and processes, the REF can provide exactly the right equipment to meet critical needs at the right time. It addresses problems much faster that anyone previously imagined possible.

The kinds of changes in structure, resourcing, and processes needed to make the REF successful challenged the conventional system and assumptions. As such, it created an opportunity for the Army to redesign its acquisition processes. The organization is converting what started as an asset for short-term agility into an asset for long-term agility that will benefit the Army for years to come.

Part II describes what agility means in the public sector and outlines what it takes to create an agile organization.

Component 3: Workforce and Culture

At the foundation of the performance anatomy of any organization is its workforce: the people, their culture, their capabilities, and their attitudes.

Lasting change in any organization begins at the top, with leadership. Many public sector leaders are in a quandary, trying to keep one foot in today so they can continue to meet their basic mission, while placing the other foot out into tomorrow so they can be prepared for whatever comes next. They must balance the discipline to drive today's mission in a reduced-cost environment with an innovation-friendly perspective for understanding tomorrow's challenges and opportunities.

The challenges don't stop there. Leadership also has to create an environment where the workforce can thrive, both today and in the future. All employees need the opportunity to develop new skills and competencies and to become more connected with their customers. There must be systems for maintaining High Performance.

A big step toward creating a future-ready workforce and a new culture focused on priorities and customers is changing how you measure performance of both processes and people. Sound targets and associated metrics provide for more open communication, the basis for evaluating how the organization is doing and what it can do better. A workforce responds to performance metrics and targets that are aligned to strategic goals, and monitored and rewarded by leadership. People will respond positively when they understand how their individual contributions affect the greater outcomes.

Part III presents a discussion of workforce and culture.

Finding the Leverage Points

Rather than addressing the full scope of High Performance, this book focuses on helping you answer every leader's first question: *where do we start?* Parts I, II, and III focus on the high-leverage points in each component of a Performance anatomy: Operational Excellence, agility, and workforce and culture. Part IV addresses the overarching task of tying all the pieces together. (The answer is simpler than you might think: you can get the shift started in the right direction by using strategic planning as the critical lever for all three ingredients.)

The need to build a robust anatomy for higher performance has never been greater. Everyone knows just how high the stakes are these days for government at all levels. Budgets across the board are being pinched. Priorities are shifting constantly with changes in public sentiment crises at home and abroad. *Not* changing, given the reality of the New Normal, is not an option.

In the prologue, we promised that creating a High Performance organization will help you reduce costs by at least 10–20% while improving quality and speed at the same time. Achieving that promise will be easier than you might think, as demonstrated by the many forward-thinking public sector organizations we highlight in the following chapters and the practical, pragmatic methods described throughout this book.

PART I

LEADING THE WAY TO OPERATIONAL EXCELLENCE

INTRODUCTION TO PART I

If you've followed business trends over the past few decades, you know that Operational Excellence is the most recent incarnation of the movement that began in the early 1980s with methods like quality improvement, total quality management, and Lean Six Sigma. The goals of this movement were and still are to help an organization do a better job of doing what it exists to do—provide some kind of product or service to someone who needs it (the customer). "Better" is traditionally defined in terms of effectiveness (delivering more of what your customers want or need) and efficiency (doing so in less time with less cost and waste).

In the private sector, improvement expertise is now common; it is less common in the public sector, and the level of maturity in managing improvement varies greatly among organizations. Some public organizations have had improvement programs that started and stopped depending on funding cycles or shifts in leadership, or they lived short lives for a host of other reasons. It seems they have to keep starting over, almost from scratch each time. Improvement programs in other public organizations may have had medium or even strong success in one area or unit but are struggling to gain broader traction and buy-in throughout the entire organization.

There are a lot of resources out there that can help. There is a growing body of knowledge—available in a variety of formats (books, courses, more formal collaborations, and consulting, to name a few)—about how to implement the components of Operational Excellence effectively in the public sector.

Of all the issues you will have to tackle, the past decades have taught us that—particularly in the public sector—effective improvement begins and ends with **strategic alignment**. You and your leadership team need to be able to link specific projects, initiatives, training, and job responsibilities to your most important organizational objectives. Building such connections is the way to make sure that what is important to your organization reflects what is important to your customers.

This section of the book addresses the strategic alignment of Operational Excellence activities:

- Developing a focus on customers and distinguishing that from a focus on other stakeholders (Spotlight A)

- Identifying the key operational gaps that block progress toward strategic goals (Chapter 2)

- Developing an appropriate mix and balance of projects, decisions, and other efforts to drive progress toward closing the strategic gaps (Chapter 3)

Recommendation: Start with an assessment

No matter where your organization falls on the implementation spectrum— just starting out or in the midst of a program that seems to be flourishing—it is wise to start with an assessment of the maturity level of your improvement program and the readiness of your organization. Use interviews, surveys, and direct observation to gather performance data so you can evaluate specifically where your workforce needs the most help, which policies or practices are helping and which are hindering progress, where you might need some outside expertise, and so on.

Special thanks to Nate Bull, Tim Collins, and Shubber Ali for help in developing the chapters in Part I.

Spotlight A

Do You Know Who Your Customers Are?

Every modern performance improvement method is based on a central premise: that customers are the only people who can tell us if we are delivering "quality." We can therefore judge the value of what we deliver only if we know who our customers are, what they want and need, and what they expect of us. Part of any mission should be getting better at filling customer wants, needs, and expectations.

This raises a crucial question: *do you know who your customers are?* Getting a clear answer about who is and isn't a customer is not a trivial issue.

The question is answered relatively easily in the private sector: customers are the people who pay money for a product or service. To stay in business and please shareholders with high returns, a company must please its customers. The answer is a bit murkier in the public sector. Except in cases where users must pay fees, agency "revenue" comes from a federal or state budget, not directly from someone who uses the agency's services. Departments and agencies believe that to stay in "business" they must please a lot of people *besides* those who directly use their services, including appointed and elected officials, politicians, taxpayers, and regulators.

For the purpose of improvement, you have to make a clear distinction between **customers**, the direct users of your services or products who are the reason why your organization exists, and **stakeholders**, people who are not users but who can influence or in other ways have a stake in your products or services.

Both groups are important to an organization, but not in the same way:

- **Customers determine quality.** It is customers who place a value on services and products. It is their needs that determine what an organization should be delivering. It is how you perform in relation to customer needs that indicates where you need to improve and where you don't. Customer feedback should influence how you define what constitutes and ideal product or service, and the processes used to deliver them.

- **Stakeholders influence your work, but do not use your products or services themselves.** They have a vested interest in or can influence the inputs to, the activities within, or the outputs of a process. Some stakeholders determine budgets, which affects your organization's ability to meet your customers' expectations. Some set policies and statutes that govern the legal limits of *how* your organization operates, the control mechanisms. Other stakeholders can nominate and appoint officials to oversee the administration of your organization and potentially challenge its practices or leadership. Some stakeholders will scrutinize the quality of services your public organization provides and present a critique (public or private) of your work. But since stakeholders do not use your products and services, their wishes have to take a backseat to what your customers say.

For example, if your organization provides aerospace engineering services for the U.S. Department of Defense, your customers are the people who will fly, service, and maintain the aircraft (the pilots and maintenance crew) plus the people who need that aircraft to perform a particular type of mission. Everyone else—Congress, generals, admirals, and, in this case, the public— is a stakeholder.

One reason for making the distinction between stakeholders and customers should be obvious from the definition: when it comes to evaluating what your organization does and why that's important, it is customer opinions that matter more than anything else. A more subtle reason for considering customer opinions first is that making your customers happy is the way to keep your stakeholders happy. Congressional representatives are *stakeholders* who represent their constituencies, some of whom might be your *customers*. Typically, they have no reason to get involved in your organization's business unless there is an interest of importance to their home district, or they learn that one of *their* customers (a constituent) is upset with you. Keep their constituents happy, and you keep an elected official happy. In the end, by better serving your real customers effectively—as demonstrated by delivering better outcomes, quality, and value—your organization will likely meet the needs of your stakeholders as well.

Differentiating Customers from Stakeholders

To illustrate the differences between customers and stakeholders, several examples at the federal government level are shown in Table B. Since the organizations in the examples are all parts of the U.S. government, anyone who resides in this country is a constituent of a sort. The question is who counts as a customer and who counts as a stakeholder in terms of driving improvements or exerting authority or other kinds of influence. For federal government organizations, assume that the general public and elected representatives, though not listed in the table, are always stakeholders.

Table B: Differentiating Customers from Stakeholders

	FEMA	NIH	U.S. Army
Customers	People and communities in need of emergency services	Americans with health issues, medical professionals, researchers	U.S. citizens, U.S. allies
Stakeholders	U.S. Dept of Homeland Security, other federal organizations, local and state elected officials from affected areas, local emergency response teams	U.S. Dept. of Health and Human Services, federal and local elected officials, health care organizations, researchers	U.S. Dept of Defense, other federal government organizations, military contractors, elected officials
Comparison to private sector	Combines functions of a home insurance company and a building contractor; payment is made in exchange for both insurance and delivery of services, when insurance is necessary	Follows an investment model, one in which the investors (taxpayers) provide money in hopes of returns (a cure or new disease prevention method)	Similar to a private security company. People pay taxes in exchange for protection, safety, and maintenance of order

Another way to sort stakeholders from customers is to take a **process view**. Look at the output that your internal operations and processes produce, and then ask yourself who ultimately receives that output. There is a very simple process analysis tool called SIPOC (pronounced "sigh-pock") that comes in handy. The initials stand for the five elements of any process: Suppliers who provide the Inputs that go through the Process, generating Outputs that go to Customers. These five elements are often presented in a diagram like the one shown in Figure 3.

Figure 3: Sample SIPOC Diagram (Process for Congressional Responses)

Suppliers	Inputs	Process	Outputs	Customers
• Congress-people • Congress-ional staffers	• Letters	Review Reqmnt. ▼ Determine Action Office ▼ Forward to Action Office ▼ Action Office develops response ▼ Action Office forwards response ▼ Review response ▼ Approve response ▼ Deliver response	• Responses	• Constituents • Congress-people

Driving higher performance requires a deep understanding of the specific output requirements of all the customers of a process. To minimize costs while maximizing outcomes, you need to ensure that the design and capability of your processes are linked to what customers recognize and value— no more, no less. This is a key insight in eliminating waste and its related cost while not blindly jeopardizing critical process outcomes.

The Price of Not Focusing on Customers

When we don't take the time to figure out what our customers want, it becomes really difficult to provide the value they want. When we don't incorporate the needs of the customer into our process design, it *guarantees* that we will spend a lot of time and energy trying to solve even more problems.

Clearly, public service organizations must balance the needs of both customers and stakeholders. By recognizing the relationship between customers and stakeholders, organizations can more effectively evaluate and weigh the risks of a new policy or change.

Identifying Customers and Their Needs

Hundreds of books and other resources will tell you how to identify your customers, understand their needs, and design products, services, and processes to better meet those needs. But at a fundamental level, becoming customer-focused is as easy as asking some simple questions:

- Who are the customers for this service or product?
- What do they want? What value are they looking for?
- Where are we meeting, exceeding, or falling short of customer expectations?
- Which gaps are most important to address first?

To each of these questions, you need to tack on a critical follow-up: *how do we know?* Many organizations make assumptions about who their customers are, what they want, and where the biggest problems in delivery, products, and services are, only to discover later that they've gotten it wrong. That is because the needs of customers change over time and vary by geography, socioeconomic level, and many other factors. Often, assumptions are either wrong or apply only to some segment of your customers. To make a decision you can be confident about, you need to **talk to your customers** to verify their needs and priorities.

As you become more experienced in working with customers, you get more sophisticated about the methods you use. Here is a quick preview of the kinds of issues you will need to tackle.

1. Identify Your Customers

As discussed earlier, a customer is a person or group who directly depends on and uses your organization's services or products. A person or group who does not directly use your product or service is not a customer. These people or groups may be stakeholders with influence or a vested interest in what your organization does, but for the purposes of designing processes and outcomes, they are not in the same category as customers.

Look at the people and groups your organization currently considers as customers. Are they all direct users of your product or service? If not, they may be stakeholders but are not true customers.

2. Develop Methods for Getting Information about Customers

Information about who your customers are, what they want and need, what frustrates them, and what *their* goals are will help you run your organization more effectively. Every organization needs to master two basic techniques of obtaining customer information, though the balance in how the two are used will vary.

- **Voice of the Customer** (VOC) techniques are used to understand what your current customers need and want. VOC methods are labeled as either passive (the information comes to your organization through your usual contacts with customers) or active (resulting from specific efforts to seek out customer contact). Some of the methods in both categories are summarized in Figure 4.

Figure 4: Voice of the Customer Methods

Voice of the Customer Methods

Passive		Active
Internal and external data	Listening post	Research methods
• Existing customer/ client information • Industry experts • Secondary data • Competitors	• Complaints • Customer service representatives • Billing • Accounts receivable • Collections	• Focus groups • Interviews • Surveys

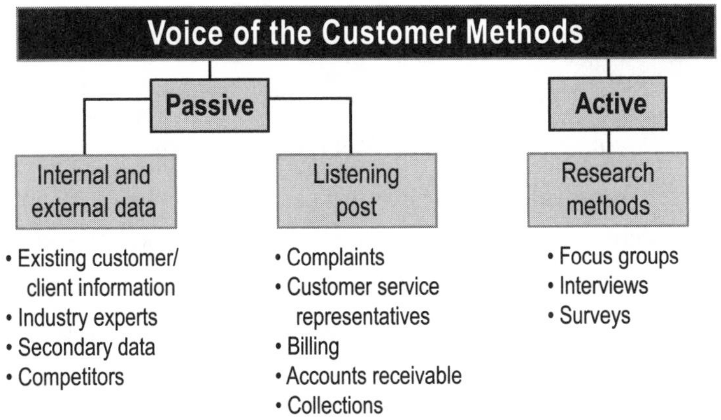

- **Heart of the Customer** (HOC) is a term we use to represent methods that go beyond the kind of statistical understanding of customer needs that comes from traditional VOC methods. HOC techniques are used to better understand the customer experience with your product or service so that you gain a comprehensive understanding of how your customers use your service or product and why they are delighted, satisfied, or frustrated. HOC methods are the best way to get the kinds of insights that can lead to innovations.

One reason for using HOC techniques is summed up in a quote attributed to Henry Ford: "If I had asked people what they wanted, they would have said faster horses."Customers can articulate their likes and dislikes with your current service or product but won't comment on needs or issues they don't associate with existing offerings or potential innovations in your field. That's why you need to go beyond what customers tell you voluntarily (passive VOC techniques), and what you learn by asking them about what they want or how they feel (active VOC techniques), to uncover opportunities for reinventing your services and products.

One of the most useful HOC approaches is **ethnographic research**, based on the tools of anthropology. You observe customers trying to perform an activity associated with your product or service and then apply that knowledge to developing new ideas that will make it easier for customers to achieve their goals. This approach exposes customer challenges, needs, and frustrations that would not come to light by any other means.

Some organizations are also using CRM (customer relationship management) tools and techniques to enhance their VOC and HOC methods. CRM systems allow organizations to compile and organize customer data more effectively than they could in the past.

3. Make Operational Changes to Better Serve Customers

To deliver more value, you have to become customer-focused in action as well as intent. Along the way, you will need to answer the following questions:

- What kinds of data collection systems do we need to maintain contact with our customers?

- Who will analyze the customer data?

- How will the data on customers be integrated into our strategic and operational planning?

- How can we ensure that departments take actions based on the customer data?

- What will it take to make our decisions more customer-focused and ensure they stay that way?

Aligning Your Organization to Customers

Professing that your organization will be customer-focused is much different from *making* it customer-focused. Only the leadership level of an organization has the authority to establish new policies and practices that will provide employees with the customer information they need to make decisions and get them to act on that information accordingly. In fact, a customer-centric approach will succeed only if leaders demonstrate an interest in customers in their own work. Discussions of customers and their needs, and how well your organization is doing in meeting those needs, should be a priority in management meetings.

For example, if a direct report comes to you with an idea for improvement or change, your first questions should be "What do our customers want?," "How will this help them?," and "Where's the data?" If there isn't existing information to answer those questions, it is your responsibility to pave the way for your direct reports to get it.

Small but critical changes in work practices, like asking those three questions, will start to build awareness and a greater focus on customers in your organization. As that focus develops, so will your ability to deliver more value.

CHAPTER 2

Aligning Outputs to Desired Outcomes

Making sure that what your organization does will get you where you want to go

You've probably heard or read the new language popping up in discussions about the responsibilities of senior leadership—how leaders need to adopt an "enterprise view" of their organization, or need to look at their organization "end to end" to achieve "alignment."

The emerging discipline of organizational alignment has developed in recognition of a simple fact of life: devoting time and effort to developing world-class processes won't have the impact you're looking for if the pieces of the organization as a whole don't fit together seamlessly.

For example, the former acting CEO of a federal agency knew the agency's two-fold mission quite well: lead the nation in fostering civic engagement through service and volunteering, and foster innovation to address our most pressing problems. The CEO and her leadership team could see great challenges for their agency. First on the list was how to expand the agency's impact under the then-new Serve America Act, given that the organization was already challenged in terms of its workload.

The agency leadership knew that one of the best ways to expose inefficiency and misalignments at a departmental or organizational level was to conduct an **enterprise analysis**, which means looking at what it takes to deliver the core work of an organization (the work that defines why the organization exists). An enterprise analysis takes a macro view of how that core work gets done as it flows through the organization and identifies the internal and external influences that affect the process, such as guidelines, policies, information, and customer and stakeholder requests. This agency was particularly interested in how outside agencies, state and local governments, and nonprofits were affecting their organization's ability to build a world-class service and volunteering organization.

By looking at the flow of work across the organization, the leadership team realized:

- The agency was striving to satisfy an unusually large number of stakeholders, including the White House and the U.S. Office of Management and Budget. Each stakeholder organization was affected by its own set of complex influences.

- Getting alignment to build a community of volunteers was complicated because the agency operates primarily through a holding-company structure. Each of its independent "business units"—AmeriCorps, VISTA, and others—has its own policies and values.

- The agency was delivering inconsistent outcomes to citizens because (a) its operations were fractured—different portions of the work were done by groups that had little or no contact with each other, leading to inefficiency, gaps, and duplication of effort, and (b) the organization had an ad hoc approach to handling high-profile initiatives that should have been more systematically managed.

To address these issues, the leadership team faced two challenges: First, the agency had to focus more on building stronger relationships and bonds with both the people who fund the agency and the people and organizations that performed the agency's volunteer placement work. Internally, this was called "strengthening the life-cycle connection," and it was directed toward national service participants, grantees, and sponsors. Second, the agency needed to improve the efficiency and consistency of its operations.

Some key recommendations resulting from the analysis are captured in Figure 5 (next page).

Figure 5: Recommendations from the Enterprise Analysis

The agency leadership credits enterprise analysis with allowing them to (a) better align outcomes, priorities, and operational capabilities, (b) identify leading practices, and (c) create a framework within which to develop organization and management recommendations.

The challenge that this agency faced is typical for public sector leaders: to align and coordinate activities within (and sometimes beyond) their official span of control in a way that enhances, not restricts, their organization's ability to accomplish its goals. As this agency discovered, the enterprise analysis was an invaluable tool for this purpose because it exposed exactly where the agency was misaligned, both internally and in relation to other governmental and non-governmental organizations. The analysis led to insights that likely never would have surfaced otherwise. The symptoms of misalignment were there for anyone to see, but it was the enterprise analysis that brought those symptoms to the fore so they could be recognized and acted on.

Our purpose in this chapter is two-fold: First, to help you understand that doing some form of enterprise analysis is no longer optional—it is a must-have for driving Operational Excellence. Second, to introduce you to a type of enterprise analysis that we call Prime Value Chain Analysis, so you can see the type of work involved and the benefits and insights to be gained.

Keeping the Links

The challenge of achieving alignment is difficult for every organization, especially in the public sector where organizations are often part of a tangled web of stakeholder communities with unique and competing needs. Though government organizations appear to operate independently, with agencies setting their own missions, core functions, and capabilities, they are actually interconnected with many sister agencies, councils, task forces, non-governmental organizations, and nonprofit organizations. Many of these sister groups operate as providers of information or services, are recipients of the organization's work, or both. Sorting out these relationships and how all the pieces have to fit together to achieve peak efficiency and effectiveness is why enterprise analysis is such a critical component of Operational Excellence in the public sector.

The path from strategy to execution is shown in Figure 6.

Figure 6: Achieving Strategic Alignment

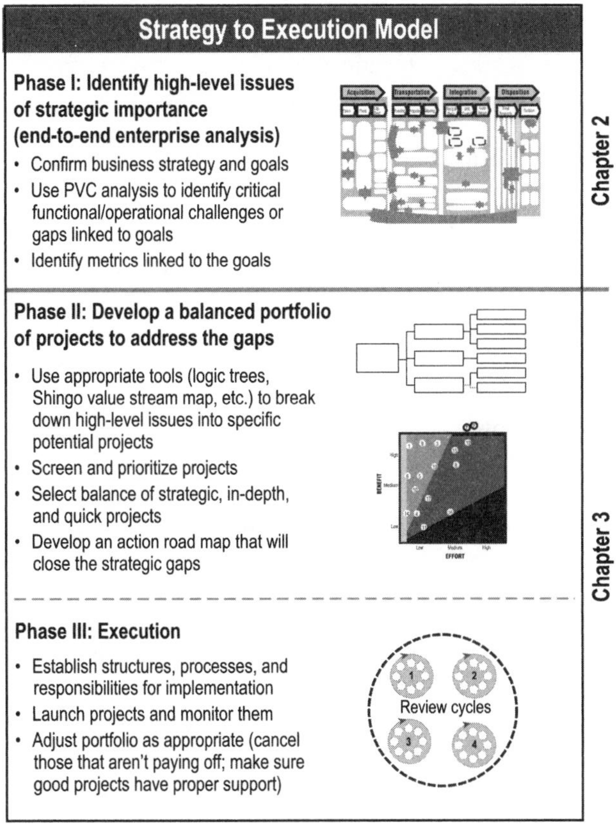

Strategy to Execution Model

Phase I: Identify high-level issues of strategic importance (end-to-end enterprise analysis)

- Confirm business strategy and goals
- Use PVC analysis to identify critical functional/operational challenges or gaps linked to goals
- Identify metrics linked to the goals

Chapter 2

Phase II: Develop a balanced portfolio of projects to address the gaps

- Use appropriate tools (logic trees, Shingo value stream map, etc.) to break down high-level issues into specific potential projects
- Screen and prioritize projects
- Select balance of strategic, in-depth, and quick projects
- Develop an action road map that will close the strategic gaps

Phase III: Execution

- Establish structures, processes, and responsibilities for implementation
- Launch projects and monitor them
- Adjust portfolio as appropriate (cancel those that aren't paying off; make sure good projects have proper support)

Review cycles

Chapter 3

The first phase describes how leadership can come to agree on priorities.

The second phase concerns identifying a range of projects, initiatives, and decisions that will move the needle on those priorities.

The last phase is about getting the right structures in place to execute that portfolio of efforts. This chapter focuses on Phase I; the other two phases are tackled in the next chapter.

Phase I: Why Do an Enterprise Analysis?

The first phase of the process for developing projects and initiatives linked to strategic goals is the kind of enterprise analysis just described above. Organizations that have never done an enterprise analysis may not realize how valuable it can be and may be tempted to skip this step. But doing so carries a number of risks: without an enterprise analysis of some form, government organizations are more likely to miss opportunities to close strategic gaps, will under-utilize resources by deploying them on "local" problems, and are more likely to allow strategic priorities to become obscured over time by inflexible functional structures and bureaucracy.

Looking at a public service outcome from an enterprise-level perspective lets you see not only how each department, functional unit, or organization contributes to that outcome but also whether the interactions among these units have a positive or negative impact. It is these interactions that can fuel friction between groups. For example, do the actions of one group contradict or compete with the efforts of another group? Are two agencies providing essentially the same service in the same community? Do members of the public know who's helping them? Or do they confuse the programs of one agency with another?

Mike Kirby, former deputy undersecretary for business transformation in the U.S. Army, summed it up this way:

> When you look enterprise-wide, look at value, you're going to learn a lot about what your organization is. You'll see impediments and processes that don't work. This is situational awareness—a tactical term that implies it's important to know what friendly and enemy forces are doing. . . . But actually it's often more difficult for a leader to know what the other friendly forces

are doing. I see so much time wasted with leaders just trying to find out what's going on so they can issue the right order. We've invested a lot in situational awareness in the military sense. Now it's time to do that for the business side.

Without a method for examining how the organization gets its work done—delivers on its mission—it is nearly impossible for senior leaders to identify the barriers and needs that are preventing their organization from achieving higher levels of performance. Taking the time to unravel that enterprise complexity and to develop an enterprise view of their organizations is eye-opening for many leaders. The best method we've found for doing an enterprise analysis is called **Prime Value Chain (PVC) analysis.**

Prime Value Chain:
A Powerful Picture of an Enterprise

As leaders in the military know, they must always be aware of how their unit's work fits into the larger picture if the mission as a whole is to succeed. This applies at every level, from a complete battle strategy to a single operation. For example, a platoon leader can look at a map and see the platoon's target hilltop surrounded by other pieces of property for which other platoon leaders are going to be responsible.

Getting that vision of the bigger picture is common in military operations but is rarely seen in non-military situations, in part because of some very real challenges:

- Government organizations perform their work through a series of vast and complex processes

- Additional complexity comes from organizational structures matrixed within and across departments; lines of authority and reporting aren't always clear

- Departments and agencies can have different perspectives on success and, therefore, different views of strategic gaps

- Departments and agencies often lack the ability to focus on the critical few strategic performance gaps, often because their attention is consumed in fighting tactical fires

- Causes, sources, and drivers of gaps in strategic performance are often unclear

These challenges can be overcome, and that's where enterprise analysis comes in. It helps you map out the "target hilltops" that belong to each of your organization's units, and often those of units outside your organization as well. It does this by examining the **value chain**, the interconnected processes that deliver your organization's principal outcomes.

The actual mechanism for conducting PVC analysis is not complicated, though successful execution relies on having people experienced with this types of analysis (whether from inside or outside your organization). The effort is similar to constructing a complete picture with incomplete pieces (see Figure 7).

Figure 7: Using PVC Analysis to Identify All Pieces of the Puzzle

A PVC analysis identifies the component pieces of your operations . . .

. . . then shows how they fit into the bigger picture, exposing structural gaps that are hindering performance.

We'll go into the details of performing a PVC analysis a little later in this chapter. First we wanted to give you an example of how it works so you can appreciate the bigger picture of its purpose and benefits.

Enterprise Analysis Case 1: Joint Munitions Command

As its name implies, the U.S. Army Joint Munitions Command (JMC) is the group responsible for getting ammunition in all its forms to warfighters. JMC is a small part of a broader ammunition supply chain that begins with the establishment of ammunition requirements and extends through sourcing and procurement all the way to the delivery of the right ammunition to the right people at the right time. The ammunition supply chain is huge: $2 billion a year in spend, involving dozens of commands networked together, thousands of steps, and hundreds of interconnected processes housed in scores of organizational silos.

When Brig. Gen. James Rogers (then a colonel) took command of JMC in 2006, he recognized that his organization was greatly constrained by events and decisions beyond its own arena of action and areas of responsibility. Though he technically owned only the logistics piece of the joint Department of Defense munitions delivery system, Rogers saw that the operation cut across four major functions, each operating as an independent silo (see Figure 8).

Figure 8: Ammunition Supply Chain (Historical View)

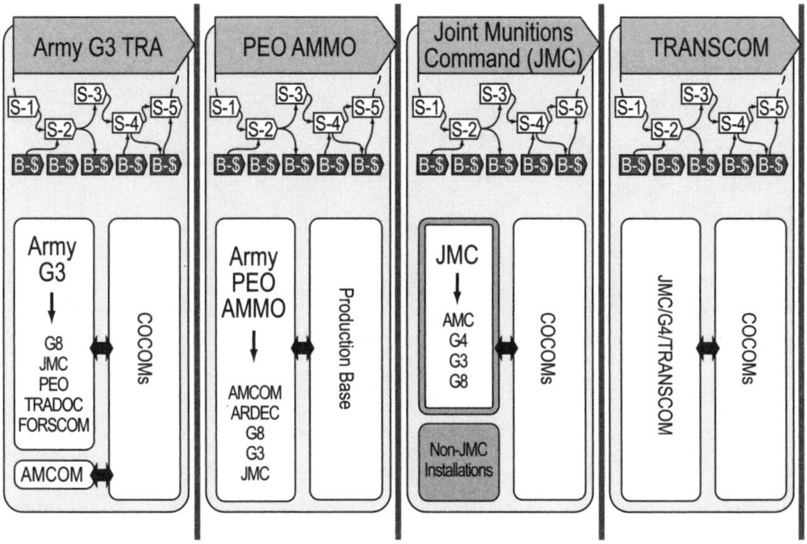

You don't need to understand the details of this diagram. What's important is to recognize that a request to get ammunition to warfighters had to travel across four silos. (Rogers's command was the third silo in the chain.) There was also significant vertical flow in multiple sub-silos before any request or material reemerged to join the "horizontal" flow of munitions toward the warfighters. Rogers had the foresight to see that his pieces of the puzzle could never be as accurate and efficient as it needed to be unless he ran his organization as part of a larger process rather than as his own private sandbox.

Rogers commissioned a network optimization study and began pulling together people from the higher ranks to help define a common picture of the organization. Never before had the leadership ranks been asked to take an enterprise view of the organization. Rogers first had to work hard to get all the leaders aligned around various aspects of the study, including a definition of the process they would use and the metrics for measuring overall success.

The resulting PVC map is shown in Figure 9.

Figure 9: PVC View of Munitions Delivery

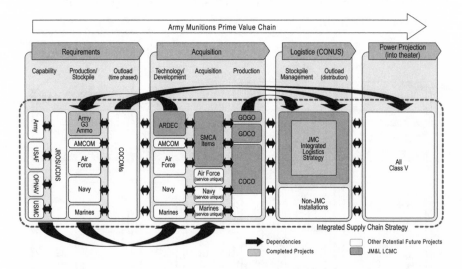

Again, don't worry about the details of the diagram. Rather, look at how the work being done is no longer defined by which functional unit is doing the work but instead by *the type of work occurring*. The heavy black arrows denote dependencies between the many organizations involved. (Be assured that a PVC diagram of your operations would have similar arrows.) Note that the connections are sometimes spaced far apart in terms of this process view of the work. Until you understand these kinds of dependencies, you can't develop effective plans for addressing them and improving efficiency throughout your value stream.

Lessons JMC Learned

A PVC diagram is important as both a *visual tool* that captures reality and a *discussion tool* that helps leaders examine the impact of strategy, mission, policies, capabilities, and interactions. Is all the work consistent with our mission? Is our strategy helping or hindering this work? Where and how do policies and other external influences come into play? Are our internal capabilities aligned with delivering our mission? Which functional units are involved and how do they interact?

For the JMC leadership and leaders of other key functions of the ammunitions delivery chain, the discussions around the PVC diagram in Figure 9 helped them visualize the flow and better understand the dynamics of this complex system. Everyone had understood that there was crosstalk among the entities, but the roles and responsibilities of the players had never really

---

PVC clarifies purpose

One key insight from the JMC analysis was that the organization was charged with two distinct functions: (1) distribution of munitions (getting the right ammunition to the right people at the right time) and (2) maintaining an archive of munitions (storing excess, outdated, or unneeded munitions).

The PVC analysis helped the leaders realize that decisions about organizational structure and function that favored either one of those functions would require them to be less efficient at fulfilling the other function. JMC leaders had to make a choice about which would be the primary function. They chose distribution, acknowledging that, in some cases, archival functions would have to take a backseat.

Because it has chosen ammunition distribution as the more important of its two key functions, JMC knows that a good business model is Walmart, a company that has mastered distribution. (Had JMC leadership decided that archiving was the organization's primary function, it may have found a more useful model in Iron Mountain, a company that specializes in records management, information destruction, and data backup.)

been laid out before in a manner that let leaders establish a common under-standing of what *should be happening where*. The lack of a shared under-standing created redundant and unnecessary work.

In this case, the PVC analysis surfaced important strategic issues with the basic business model that drove the structure of this value stream. By force of will, the Army had been able to cover the shortages that the PVC analy-sis revealed, but doing so had meant buying millions of dollars in excess munitions in some areas and under-buying in others. These inefficiencies had created problems throughout the infrastructure used to store, transport, and decommission outdated or unneeded munitions.

JMC realized that excess infrastructure and its attendant cost could be removed without adversely affecting services. These and other insights formed the basis for a change in strategy and spawned more than 20 Lean Six Sigma projects that helped implement new functionalities, build better communications between groups, and reduce input volatility. The result was a dramatic improvement in service and investment.

It should be noted that random improvement projects executed within the silos could never have exposed the system-level misalignments and func-tional disconnects that were brought to light in the JMC analysis. PVC analysis ensures that improvement projects of any kind are focused on clos-ing strategic performance gaps rather than, for example, on improving inter-nal efficiency. Though valuable, random operational improvements will likely have less impact on performance in strategically critical areas.

How to Do a PVC Analysis

There are five steps in doing a PVC analysis. Here is a quick list; details follow:

1. Define the purpose and scope

2. Conduct enterprise-focused interviews with stakeholders

3. Perform other baseline analyses

4. Create a high-level PVC diagram

5. Develop a list of high-priority targets

1. Define the Purpose and Scope

A PVC analysis can be performed at almost any level of an organization. The focus is determined by the broader context driving the PVC. To start, your executive leadership needs to identify:

- **Key business metrics to target.** Metrics should be aligned to driving the business issues that leadership needs to address and the outcomes it needs to deliver. The right metrics are the key to strengthening the organization; for example, to maintaining performance at lower cost or to expanding the capacity to take on new work.

- **Initial scope.** The scope should include the processes, business units, and resources within your organization that will be involved in analysis. Also identify partner organizations, suppliers, customer groups, and other entities *outside* your organization that affect how well you fulfill your mission. The scope of the analysis may shift as systemic issues are identified.

- **Stakeholders.** Develop a list of stakeholders (distinct from customers) that the analysis will impact, including any supporting boards or committees. This list will help you develop communication and collaboration strategies.

- **Participant roles, responsibilities, and accountabilities.** Defining roles, responsibilities, and accountabilities early in the process will bring the organizational and governance structure into focus. Identify the people and teams responsible for conducting and governing the assessment, and outline the roles and responsibilities of the assessment team members. This will make it clear who is accountable for completing the analysis.

- **Timeline and work plan.** Developing a common work plan and timeline, complete with target completion dates, helps the assessment team define the critical path for success. Identify and set dates for milestones where you will conduct progress reviews.

- **Communications plan.** Enterprise analysis helps to unite a group around common issues. You'll have a better chance of creating unity if you communicate the purpose, goals, and lessons from the analysis to the workforce. That's why it is important to identify the mechanisms that you will use for communication during the assessment. Include how information will be gathered, which people or groups will be involved in providing feedback, and how to communicate the status of the project throughout.

- **Criteria for success.** How will you know if the enterprise analysis has been successful? What do you want to accomplish through the analysis, apart from the organizational issues and business goals you want to address? Defining what success looks like up front will help the assessment team understand your intent and the lessons you hope to learn.

Keep focused on the most critical improvement opportunities required to reach mission objectives. If your leadership team hasn't already done so, get aligned on how to objectively define and measure progress on strategic objectives. What do the data and observations of the workplace reveal about why you may be struggling to meet strategic goals? Probe more deeply into any shortfalls by defining subordinate key measures and outputs.

It may help you think about your needs in three areas:

1. **Strategy.** Read the strategic plan, leaders' guidance, or any organizational strategy documents available. Identify top-level strategies you can support. Is the agency under budget pressure and thus cutting operating costs is paramount? Is the agency looking to become greener? Is there a critical strategic project where performance is lagging, where a focused improvement project could speed up a successful implementation? Is the agency's mission expanding or changing dramatically, creating an opportunity to help deal with shifting requirements?

2. **Objectives.** Once you have identified strategic priorities, outline specific objectives tied to each strategy. Is there a 10% operational budget shortfall? If so, what are the main levers? If speed, cost, or quality is an issue, you might ask if continuous process improvement (CPI) methods could help drive the needed performance gains.

3. **Operating environment.** Most agencies are experiencing some or all of the following pressures: extreme budget constraints, increasing mission requirements, increased public and Congressional scrutiny,

an aging workforce, and difficulties in implementing new programs. Understanding these environmental factors for your agency will help you make better-informed decisions when developing a project portfolio—not only what to select but what *not* to select. (For example, if there is a project that has received lots of attention and resources but has failed to make any progress, you need to decide whether to try a new approach or cancel the project and use those resources on other priorities.)

2. Conduct Enterprise-Related Interviews with Stakeholders

PVC analysis interviews explore how important factors such as strategy, mission, and policy affect stakeholder decisions, priorities, and options. Stakeholders include senior leaders who represent all parts of the value chain. You will want to ask these stakeholders questions that help to define the operational demands of your organization. (See example set of questions in the sidebar on the next page.)

3. Perform Other Baseline Analyses

Talking to representative stakeholders is just one source of information when doing a PVC analysis. Other analyses you should perform include:

- **Observe key areas of the value chain in action.** Go to the place where the core work of your organization happens, and observe. We borrow this concept from the expression used as part of Lean improvement methods, "Go to the Gemba." It means to go to the place where the work is done. This is a much richer and much more accurate source of information than simply reading protocols or standard operating procedures (SOPs).

- **Gather and analyze data.** Review process and performance documentation and data. You can gather and analyze this information with a suite of both simple and sophisticated tools, including:
  - Cross-organizational process mapping. Here, you examine how work flows back and forth between organizations. This type of analysis is particularly important in organizations whose work is highly dependent on what is done in some other organization or agency.

Example questions for an executive stakeholder interview

Here is a sampling of questions you'd want to ask of any senior leaders you contact as part of an enterprise analysis.

1. For an overview of the person's activities and responsibilities:

- What is your understanding of our mission?
- Who are your customers? What are their needs and expectations?

2. For an understanding of the process directed by the person:

- What is the output of your process?
- Who receives that output?
- What are the key activities that generate the output?
- What triggers those activities?
- Who are the key players in the process, both internal and external?
- Which groups or organizations provide input to the process?

3. For determining performance indicators:

- How do you know if the process is successful?
- How do you know if you're doing a good job? What data do you look at?
- What are the few critical skills and capabilities that your organization must do well to meet customer needs?
- What would your customers say are the greatest improvement opportunities? How would they measure your success?
- How well is the process meeting customer needs from your perspective? What are the biggest gaps?

4. To understand the challenges:

- What are the biggest challenges your organization faces or will face? What is hard to deal with? What is easy?
- What drives complexity, confusion, or ambiguity in the process?
- What changes are driving the challenges?
- What are some of the biggest opportunities for the future? Why?
- What would need to be changed to enable capturing those opportunities? Why?
- Who would disagree with your view of the opportunities? Why?

– **Complexity value stream mapping and complexity analytics.** This type of analysis looks at what it costs you to maintain the full range of products and services you offer. And we don't mean just money. It addresses the complexity of the organization and all the processes you maintain to produce all your products and services (see sidebar).

– **Cultural and maturity assessments.** Assessments help you understand your organization's readiness to take on change. Cultural assessments examine the workplace culture and how it can help or hinder the way you want to operate in the future. Maturity assessments examine how much experience different parts of your organization have with improvement and change.

Understanding the impact of complexity

Organizations are often overwhelmed by trying to be everything to everybody. Having too much variety slows down everything and increases costs across the board. For example, maintaining a service that is needed for only one month a year has an impact on the cost and efficiency of delivering the services you do every day. You may still have to provide the rarely used service, but there could be ways to minimize its impact elsewhere.

Complexity analytics help you understand how the delivery of any single product or service is affected by the delivery of all the other products and services that use any or all of the same process steps. This knowledge is critical in shaping the structure of the organization so that you can either maintain your full range of services (with greater efficiencies) or perhaps trim back on some services once you appreciate the full cost to the organization.

---

4. Create a High-Level PVC Diagram

A PVC diagram captures the basic flow of work and information between the major components of the value stream. Your goal is to develop a picture or map that shows how major activities across the scope of a broader activity or workflow are grouped, using information from the interviews and other sources. The map should capture information flow, material flow, and money flows (see Figure 10).

Figure 10: PVC Schematic

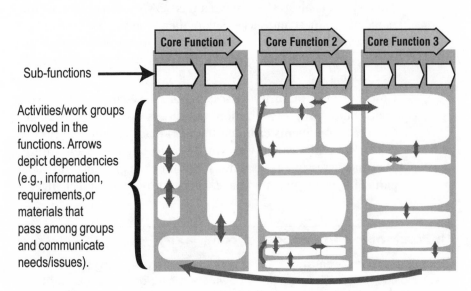

As you saw with the JMC diagram shown earlier, PVC maps will be visually complex to anyone who wasn't involved in creating then. To create this schematic, we've removed some detail from the example. Keep in mind, too, that the diagram itself is merely a by-product. The most important aspect of this work is the discussions that go on within and between departments, work groups, and other units. Those discussions not only generate the information used to create the diagram but also help the group reach agreement on priorities, the source of conflicts, and so on.

5. Develop a List of High-Priority Targets

In this synthesis stage, all the information gathered thus far is brought together to answer strategic questions, summarized in Figure 11 (next page).

As you examine the PVC diagram and review the interviews, discussions, and related sources of information, be alert for:

- **Functional duplication of effort.** Does more than one unit or sub-unit perform essentially the same work?

- Organizational "white spaces." Is there a department, unit, or staff member *not* clearly connected to the mission, products, or services the organization provides? Are there functions you should be performing that no one is now responsible for?

- **Excessive hand-offs.** How many times does any single item of work get passed back and forth between departments, units, or staff members? Is the sequence of hand-offs essential to adding the value that customers are looking for? If not, you may be able to re-sequence the work to reduce the handoffs and eliminate steps that add no value.

- **Places where the color of money changes.** Are there places where the source of funding changes in a process? This may indicate a need to look at the complexity.

- **Misalignments, disconnects, and misperceptions.** Bring representatives from the affected groups together and use the PVC diagram to "walk the process" together. Does the diagram match people's experience? Are there misalignments, disconnects, and misperceptions from one group to another?

Figure 11: Strategic Questions for a Prime Value Chain Analysis

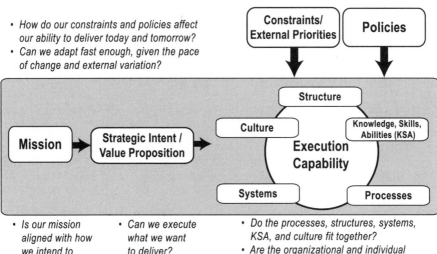

43

As you complete this analysis, think about the effect of the problems you've identified in your organization's processes. As you develop a full understanding of what needs to happen and how products and services are being delivered, you will be able to identify key process points where internal controls or requirements are inadequate or too restrictive. Also, take time to evaluate the alignment of organizational structure, linking mechanisms, and key performance drivers and the process and technologies employed.

To help build your understanding of how a PVC analysis works, here is another example.

Enterprise Analysis Case 2: Common Ground

Common Ground is a nonprofit organization in New York City that is dedicated to the elimination of homelessness. By the nature of its work, Common Ground has to connect with dozens of government agencies and other nonprofit organizations. Thanks to its Street-to-Home program, homelessness in the 20-block Times Square neighborhood has dropped by 87%.

As with any nonprofit, Common Ground must make efficient use of time and dollars. In 2008, the organization realized that the processes it was using to move clients from the street to placement were too lengthy and relied on far too many variables. The leadership wanted to identify and prioritize corrective actions to speed up the shorter-term process of placing clients in housing, including collaboration with city agencies and other partners. The leaders approached the issue as a set of long-term strategic opportunities to enhance Common Ground's overall capability.

Common Ground's challenges and needs were textbook criteria for doing an enterprise analysis:

- The organization was looking at a problem that arose from barriers that crossed internal and external boundaries.

- Operations were centered in silos.

- The structure is complex. Many services, each provided by different groups, have to be coordinated for the organization to be successful. There are also multiple external stakeholders (people and groups interested in their work, some of whom have the power to affect direction and funding), and multiple suppliers for the services.

- Because of the complexity of its operations, it was not clear why the organization was unable to achieve its goals. There was no obvious culprit.

An outside team of experts helped Common Ground perform the enterprise analysis. Their interviews with key stakeholders and the development of a PVC diagram revealed a number of barriers standing in the way of greater client placement. Delays in securing housing for the homeless resulted in numerous impacts:

- Extending the length of time needed for client placement and program coordination

- Challenges in balancing the supply of housing categories against client needs

- Excessive delays in dealing with external agencies

- Rework due to delays that required duplicate testing and overuse of scarce resources, including the resubmission of documentation confirming eligibility

Figure 12 (top of next page) shows a schematic view of Common Ground's PVC diagram and illustrates some of the problems exposed during its development. In the figure, you can identify four main steps in the delivery of the agency's core value: Enroll, Qualify, Place, and House.

As members of the leadership team discussed these problems, they developed a multi-phase plan of attack:

- Immediate steps included getting all the stakeholders aligned around the mission and vision. This was basically a communication step— getting lots of people into a room, talking about their interpretations of the mission, finding out where opinions differed or were aligned, and reaching agreement on a single interpretation of the mission.

- The biggest problems identified through the analysis were issues that could be solved with short-term actions. For example, the team was able to find ways to restructure their processes so more work could be

45

Figure 12: Common Ground's PVC Analysis (Schematic)

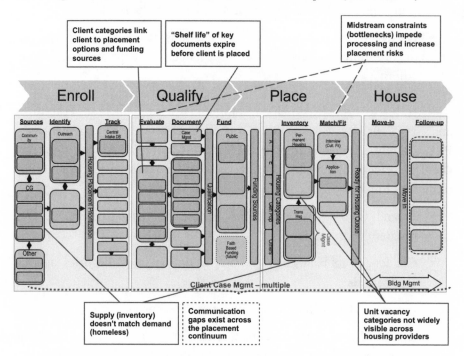

done concurrently rather than having it all done sequentially. This was crucial in cutting down the overall cycle time. Other projects took on the issue of improving documentation shelf life, the visibility of placement openings, client and stakeholder feedback, and information management.

- Longer-term projects were launched to address the problems that did not have quick fixes, including supply versus demand forecasting, managing constraints, linking clients to appropriate funding, and strengthening communications.

Work on implementing these ideas is ongoing, but Common Ground reports that it has already seen a benefit in getting staff from two key placement programs (Street-to-Home and Housing Operations) integrated as one team. The organization is also focusing on improving its performance measurement so that it can better evaluate the impact of future actions.

Top Challenges in Enterprise Analysis

An enterprise analysis can be especially challenging in some public sector organizations. Here are some areas of potential difficulty:

- **Achieving agreement on the definition of the whole process.** The value of an enterprise analysis is diminished if you don't look at the whole enterprise as broadly as you can. As the examples in this chapter show, that can sometimes include looking beyond the borders of your organization. But silos are rampant in the public sector for many reasons, including the fear of scope creep (attempting to take on something that is beyond the organization's capability to handle well) and other disincentives for paying attention to anything outside your own organization. Overcoming these cultural barriers can be difficult.

- **Defining the metrics of success.** Part of an enterprise analysis is to consider how you will know whether the analysis and the subsequent initiatives have been successful—which metrics you will use to gauge success. Equally important is deciding how you can break down those metrics into subcomponents that people at each level of the organization can use and influence.

- **Determining who owns a process.** To improve performance, you need to improve processes. To ensure that changes are implemented and maintained, you need a person—a process owner—responsible for monitoring the process performance and enforcing new methods and standards. Identifying a single process owner is challenging in the public sector because work often crosses many horizontal and vertical boundaries.

- **Getting everyone to the table.** The value of your enterprise analysis will depend on the quality of information you get. If there are many stakeholders involved, you need to bring them all into the process so that you can ask them directly what they care about. Many times, we are more comfortable relying on the historical or anecdotal memory of our "sages," but it is best to rely on data and encourage constructive dialogue with our partners.

Worth the Effort

As the examples above show, an enterprise analysis is mission-focused. Its purpose is to give leaders insights about organizational needs and priorities that are difficult if not impossible to come by through other means. Performing an enterprise analysis lets you anchor your improvement efforts, ensure strategic mission alignment, and clarify intersections and interactions among the key elements you need to address, such as strategy, policy, mission, process, and organization.

The enterprise analysis model described in this chapter has three additional benefits:

- **Creating the first links in the chain from strategy to execution.** The first steps in the PVC analysis get leadership to connect the primary element of the organization's mission (to support its service of the nation and its citizens) to the activities the organization needs to deliver on that mission.

- **Engaging executive leadership.** Change can be successfully implemented only if it has the backing, buy-in, and participation of decision makers and other influential organizational leaders. Participating in a PVC analysis gives leaders a forum for discussing *and resolving* differences in opinions about the organization's needs and priorities.

- **Generating tangible results.** Though the PVC process is designed to generate a list of priorities, the effort inevitably reveals a number of quick changes that can bring tangible results immediately. Those positive effects can be amplified as improvement initiatives tied to the organization's priories are enacted; they may include measurable improvements in organizational effectiveness and process performance (such as reduced costs, improved quality, greater speed, and reduction of risk).

Government leaders we've worked with at all levels have agreed that taking the time to develop an end-to-end view of their enterprise is eye-opening. In as little as five weeks, they gained insights that had eluded the organization for years: for example, where cross-functional gaps and barriers were putting an artificially low ceiling on their organization's performance. As leaders, they were the people with the reach and authority to change those kinds of barriers. They have also been much more confident that the actions they launched—whether strategic initiatives or formal improvement projects or quick "just-do-it" fixes—would have a direct, positive effect on the strategic gaps they were responsible for closing.

Reaching a shared understanding of how your organization works is perhaps the single most important step a leadership team can take to drive progress. Enterprise analysis is a rapid, comprehensive diagnostic that can help you get there.

CHAPTER 3

Creating an Action Road Map

Chapter 1 introduced the story of how MRAP vehicle production was accelerated from 10 units a month to 50 units a day between April and December of 2007. You don't make that kind of progress without having a very good plan for making goals a reality. In that case, there was a tremendous sense of urgency around the ramp-up—real lives were at stake.

An assessment of the MRAP processes early on identified the three biggest issues standing in the way of achieving higher MRAP production levels:

- **The complexity of the vehicle configuration.** Originally, the MRAP "vehicle" was really nine different vehicles, each done in two sizes (large and small) for five clients (the Army, Air Force, Navy, Marines, and special operations). By the time everything came together in the assembly operation, there were 1,000 variations of MRAPs that had to be produced. The great variability in configurations clogged processes along the entire production chain, from procurement to delivery.

- **Lack of supply chain alignment**. The MRAP assembly operation originally worked by having all the parts delivered at the very end of each month—a batch model of production. Batch processing is feasible if you're producing only 10 vehicles a month (requiring relatively low stock levels), but it is inefficient when you need to produce 50 vehicles each day. Velocity in any process, manufacturing or transactional, is incompatible with batch delivery of materials. If you want to work fast—and particularly if you want to work fast with high volumes— you have coordinate the timing and size of supply delivery to match the production demand.

- **Lack of a robust process for making engineering changes.** As with any product, the MRAP vehicle is subject to design changes based on lessons learned about its use in the field, new functionality requirements, and changes in materials or components. The process for implementing such engineering changes was very slow, with multiple levels of reviews and approvals needed. This slowness is workable but not ideal when dealing with low production levels but will prevent a process from achieving high production levels.

The team identified a range of improvement projects linked directly to the three issues. The final project portfolio included:

- Only projects linked directly to improving production ramp-up objectives. Potential projects that would not contribute to ramp-up were rejected, even if they promised a high return in other ways.

- A handful of full-blown Six Sigma projects, requiring the analytical rigor of the DMAIC problem-solving process (Define, Measure, Analyze, Improve, Control) and focusing on key technical issues.

- Approximately 20 Rapid Improvement Event (RIE) projects (also called Kaizen events) focused on improving plant layout and production flow. RIEs or Kaizens are projects where a team comes together for a few days or even a full week and works *only* on solving a precisely targeted problem. An RIE allows you to generate important incremental improvements very quickly and can often be replicated in other areas, as was done in this case.

- Almost 100 just-do-it projects. Among these were implementing a robust engineering change process that allowed quicker communication of changes to all parts of the production process and changes to procurement policies to better support flow (for example, to eliminate batch release of parts purchase orders).

In selecting projects, the team had no rules about the types of projects or methodologies it would consider. The only question asked was, "Is this something that directly supports the production ramp-up?"

The resulting portfolio was balanced in that it included a wide range of project types, yet it was skewed *appropriately for the situation* toward speed and production outcomes. There were no training projects, no initiatives about building long-term capability, for example.

This bias toward action and immediate impact was obviously the right choice in this case. What's important about this example is that the task force had a clear, agreed-upon goal, identified from a strategic viewpoint what would need to change to achieve that goal, and then linked its project choices to those strategies.

Picking Up the Strategy-Execution Link

When the deputy director of a large government agency was asked how his organization had been selecting and managing continuous process improvement (CPI) projects, his response was "On a hope and a prayer." His response was obviously in jest, but it makes the point that project selection can be somewhat of a mystery and that leaders often suspect they are not getting the most out of their project portfolio selection process. When pressed, this leader confided, "When we started, we had a leadership council, and we started by having selection workshops focused on key issues from our command strategic plan." He went on to say that the process broke down when they deployed it further into the organization. "Things got away from us," he admitted.

This unease is reflected in reality. All too often, project portfolios are clogged with bottom-up, departmentally focused projects and managers' pet projects that have no tie to the agency mission, strategy, objectives, or operating environment. Because the projects are likely to be unimportant or of lesser value than other potential projects, they have trouble vying for agency attention. In that kind of environment, projects often take 9 to 12 months to complete, and many peter out before completion.

Even when projects are considered "valuable," the benefit is often counted at the local level (within a silo or narrow value stream). Across a large, complex organization it is typical for hundreds of such projects to be launched despite the fact that few, if any, are interrelated—nor do they aggregate toward improving the vital few strategic objectives of the organization.

Similarly, metrics of success are dominated by activity metrics, like the number of total projects launched or completed rather than outcome-oriented metrics—the progress made toward real business objectives.

To avoid these problems, project identification and selection must come *after* agreement on strategies and priorities. A process for moving from strategy to execution was introduced in the previous chapter and is reproduced in Figure 13. The previous chapter discussed Phase I, the enterprise analysis phase, in which you identify strategic priorities. This chapter completes the strategy-to-execution links by discussing Phase II (identifying projects that will generate meaningful progress on the priorities) and Phase III (putting the structures in place to ensure execution of the projects.

Figure 13: Strategy to Execution

Phase I: Identify high-level issues of strategic importance (end-to-end enterprise analysis)

- Confirm business strategy and goals
- Use PVC analysis to identify critical functional/operational challenges or gaps linked to goals
- Identify metrics linked to the goals

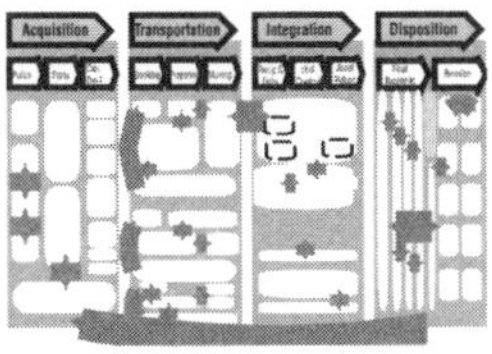

Chapter 2

Phase II: Develop a balanced portfolio of projects to address the gaps

- Use appropriate tools (logic trees, Shingo value stream map, etc.) to break down high-level issues into specific potential projects
- Screen and prioritize projects
- Select balance of strategic, in-depth, and quick projects
- Develop an action road map that will close the strategic gaps

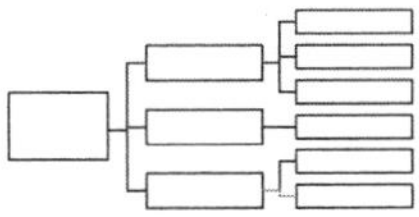

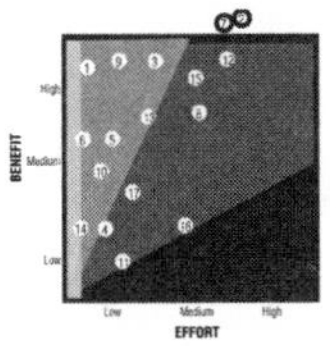

Phase III: Execution

- Establish structures, processes, and responsibilities for implementation
- Launch projects and monitor them
- Adjust portfolio as appropriate (cancel those that aren't paying off; make sure good projects have proper support)

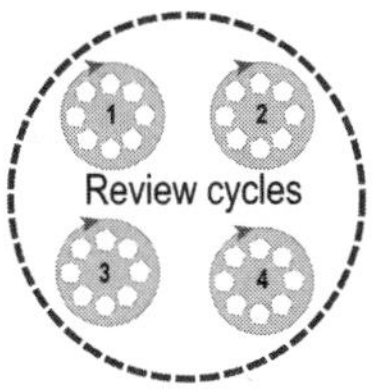

Review cycles

Chapter 3

Phase II: Developing a Balanced Portfolio

To illustrate the challenge in developing a balanced portfolio, consider the range of potential projects and issues to be explored. It may help to think about arranging them on a continuum, as shown in Figure 14.

Figure 14: Continuum of Issues for a Balanced Portfolio

	STRATEGIC ⟵				⟶ TACTICAL
	STRATEGY	**COMPLEXITY/ INNOVATION**	**BLACK BELT**	**GREEN BELT**	**GO-DO**
Scope	• Strategic issues • Organizational issues • Participation issues • Systemic issues • Solution unknown • Unbounded (potentially)	• May/may not be strategy-neutral • Product/service decisions • Systemic issues across value streams • Solution unknown	• Process issues within a value-stream • Bounded by resources/time • Solution unknown • Strategy neutral	• Small process issue within a value stream • Bounded by resources/time • Solution unknown	• Small issue within a value stream • Solution known
Area of Impact	• Corporation / Business unit	• Systemic process issues • Offering configuration • Strategy	• Broader part of a process	• Specific part of a process	• Specific, small issue
Tools	• Strategic analysis leveraging various frameworks	• Complexity analysis • Fast innovation • Strategic analysis	• DMAIC • DFLSS	• Lean • Kaizen • DMAIC	• PDCA
	Non-repetitive Issue Resolution		**Repetitive Issue Resolution**		

Project initiatives range from those addressing high-level, fairly complex problems (left side of Figure 14) to more tactical Kaizen events and basic business decisions (right side). This spectrum visually represents what we mean by a balanced project portfolio. Laying out the issues in this way will help you avoid the "silver bullet" trap: the belief that a single methodology (Lean or Six Sigma, Kaizens, Theory of Constraints, etc.) can be used to address all issues an organization faces. Also, it reinforces the principle that it is a waste of resources to devote more effort to a problem than it needs; for example, launching a Black Belt or Six Sigma project for something that is a just-do-it level. Conversely, you'll have trouble making progress on complicated issues if you restrict yourself to Green Belt or Kaizen types of projects.

Understanding the issues facing the organization as a continuum is also important in assigning accountability down to the teams responsible for improvement of the metric in question. Leadership recognition that this continuum exists is key to execution.

Identify Potential Projects

In the early years of quality improvement, project identification and selection came largely from open brainstorming by everyone from senior management to frontline workers. That approach was great for generating a lot of creative energy, but the result was a mishmash of projects with uncertain value. That's why the emphasis today is on using methods that help you establish and maintain direct links between the actions you select and the strategic goals you identified.

A wide range of tools and methods can be used for this purpose, far too many to cover in this book. In our view, a list of potential areas for improvement is best developed as an outcome of an enterprise analysis, as discussed in the previous chapter. That's the best way to ensure that the ideas you decide to propose are problems or opportunities linked to strategy or operational goals, and agreed on by top leadership (presuming it was involved in the enterprise analysis).

However, it's likely that the ideas emerging from the enterprise analysis will need further development to identify specific projects. Two underutilized tools we recommend for this purpose are **logic trees** and **Shingo value stream maps**:

- **Logic trees** are useful when you already have a good understanding of how the issues you've identified manifest themselves in your organization. They will let you divide a large, often seemingly insoluble problem into manageable components for action. This tool is useful for identifying projects that are linked to strategic issues. You end having a good idea of the *set of projects* needed to move the needle on an important issue.

- **Shingo value stream maps** are more effective when problems are only vaguely defined, and you need more detail about the sources or locations of waste, inefficiencies, and other hindrances. This tool is most often used for identifying projects that are linked to tactical issues. Using this method, you have a better understanding of where in your processes there are problems impeding efficiency or effectiveness.

Logic trees

A logic tree is a diagram used to identify which parts of a strategic issue you can address to have the biggest impact. The diagram starts with any strategic priority and then looks at increasingly detailed components. You end up with a number of problem statements and eventually with hypotheses that can be proved or disproved.

The key to a useful logic tree is designing the right structure. You want to think **MECE** (pronounced *me-CE*)—Mutually Exclusive, Collectively Exhaustive. MECE means that the categories you identify do not overlap (are mutually exclusive) but when viewed as a whole (collectively) cover all aspects of the issue (are exhaustive). Maintaining the MECE construct allows your logic to flow from problem to solution and on to results.

Figure 15 (next page) illustrates how the problem of late-arriving flights could be subdivided level by level until the team reached something actionable. The airline in this example identified one problem: an aggregate 14% of its flights were arriving late (representing "100% of the problem"). In Figure 15, the lateness is identified as a single problem the airline wanted to solve. Participants in the effort looked at the problem by region (the numbers add up to 100%), then by city, and then by type of problem. From this analysis, it was clear that the biggest impact would come from addressing the problems in the Northeast. While management couldn't do much about the weather, they could institute policies around schedules for times when weather problems are likely. They could also set up teams to study maintenance and other issues.

There is no limit to the variety of perspectives or stratification levels that can be investigated with a logic tree. How you choose to subdivide your issue depends on the insights of experts who are familiar with that type of problem. The experts may suspect the source of problems; you can turn their ideas into hypotheses and create a division on the logic tree that will help you test it. For example, suppose the most experienced people agreed that problems were worse at certain times of the year or month. That opinion represents a hypothesis that there are seasonal effects. On the tree, you could divide the problem by units of time or seasons or by fiscal quarter, for example.

Figure 15: Example Logic Tree

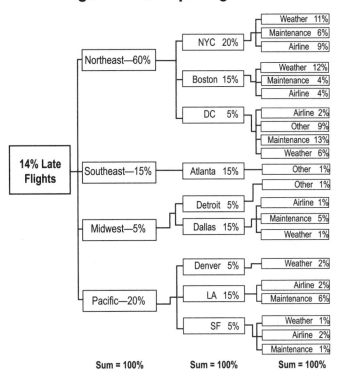

Shingo value stream map

Many strategic opportunities identified in the PVC analysis are not ready for a logic tree analysis because the underlying issues are not clear. An alternative tool you can use in such cases is the Shingo value stream map (Shingo VSM). Value stream maps were first introduced as a component of the PVC analysis discussion in Chapter 2. Value stream maps capture the flow of work across a set of processes that deliver the value your organization exists to provide. There are various forms of value stream maps; the Shingo style captures process actions in more detail than is typical of other types of maps. That detail is helpful in tracking down the sources of excess delay and cost in a process (see Figure 16, next page).

At the top level, a Shingo VSM shows from four to six of the highest-order process steps for the area. Beneath each step are listed the subprocesses that culminate in achieving the major process step. The map captures data that allows you to identify inefficiencies, including the following:

- Long process lead times

- Non-value-added process steps and operations

- Rework, expediting, and constant troubleshooting

- Frequent divergence from defined processes and standards

- Disparate, disconnected support systems

- Symptoms of problems whose true costs are buried in financial statements (dispersed across several cost categories, for example)

- Deteriorating budgets

Figure 16: Shingo Value Stream Map

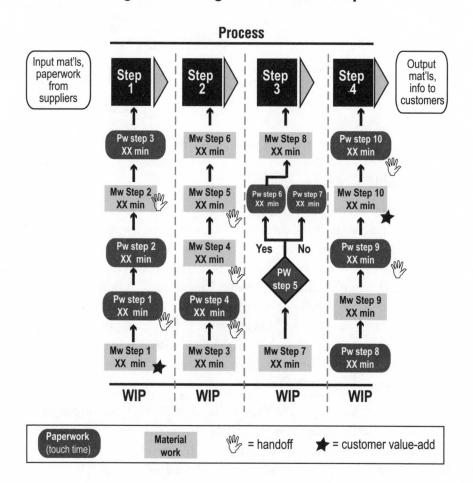

The work that goes into developing the map and creating a visual depiction of both value and waste in the subprocesses gives you a deeper insight into problems and lets you develop solutions much more quickly. This analysis helps you understand the levers and interactions among the different elements of the value chain, which is critical to eliminating non-value-added activity and optimizing efficiency.

Define, Rank, and Validate Opportunities

The ultimate goal of the Balanced Portfolio phase is to create a road map, a plan that identifies the improvement initiatives the leadership team believes are most critical for driving performance and closing strategic gaps. The road map should include the timeline, sequencing, resources, stakeholders, and sponsors, and should address other requirements as well.

Before getting to the road map, however, you need to know which of the many possible projects to work on. If you took the outcome from a typical project selection process and then evaluated the ideas based on benefit versus effort, you'd end up with a graph something like Figure 17.

Figure 17: Project Selection without Filters

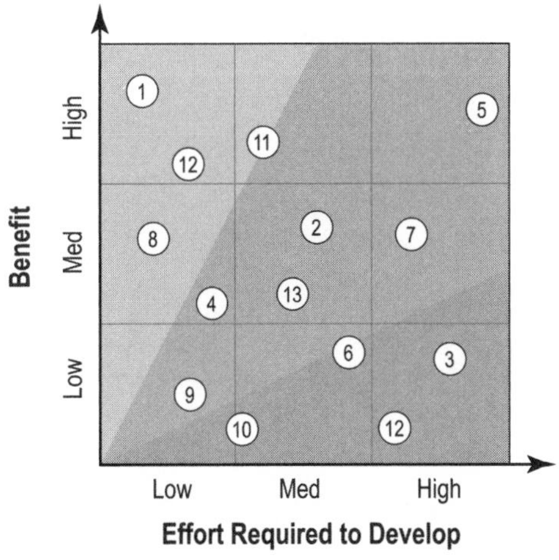

When projects are selected without any filters, you end up with a mix of projects representing a range of benefit and effort.

What you should be aiming for instead is a process that lets you filter ideas based on their likely contribution to solving the problem and the amount of effort needed to achieve that benefit (Figure 18). Filtering the projects in this way also helps you match the right methodology to each different project type.

Figure 18: Prioritized Project Analysis

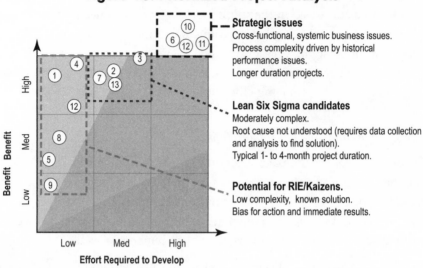

To develop the prioritized value agenda and road map represented in Figure 18, you start with the dozens of opportunities (each differing in strategic impact and amount of effort required), identified through a logic tree, Shingo VSM, or other analysis. Next, you screen projects against a set of criteria to determine which should get priority on the road map. Typical criteria include:

- Strength of the link between the project and targeted strategic or operational issues

- Level of effort required

- Stakeholder and sponsor support of this initiative

- Number of existing projects focused on this issue

- Organizational pushback

- Resources (overlaps, competing demands, specialized needs, etc.)

- Change management (preparing for change, fighting resistance, aligning policy, etc.)

- Required leadership roles (sponsors, stakeholders, process participants; roles in removing barriers, making decisions, resolving conflicts, etc.)

You also need to identify the benefits and costs of the potential projects, so that you can estimate the return on investment (Table C).

Table C: Evaluating Benefits versus Costs

Types of Benefits	Types of Costs
• $$ savings • Cost avoidance • Sustainability benefits • Safety or quality improvements • Customer satisfaction • Employee satisfaction	• Costs to solve the problem (out-of-pocket, capital, resource investment) • Time to implement • Risks • Opportunities (won or lost)

Develop the Road Map

Once you have sorted the ideas based on their cost and impact, the next step is to convert the list of projects to a road map (some organizations call it a playbook) that spells out which projects will be worked on in what sequence. That sequence will rely in part on the cross-process and cross-initiative dependencies: what is happening in other processes or efforts internally or externally that could affect the timing of your projects. Each opportunity is then force-ranked using comparison techniques.

This effort yields a robust, prioritized list of improvement initiatives and an understanding of their optimal sequence. Before constructing the road map, it is critical to validate the priorities with senior leadership. Typically, this activity is undertaken in an executive workshop so that key leaders have the ability to shape the implementation plan before its execution.

The executive workshop also provides a forum for leaders to confirm their shared commitment to the path forward, resource allocation, and direct lines of communication necessary for execution. It's important that the workshop not be the first time the leadership team receives this information, as it should have by this time been vetted in one-on-one conversations with each key stakeholder.

Once you have leadership approval of the prioritized opportunities, you can construct the final road map. It should include the following information for each project: the business cases, team assignments, sequencing, and a plan for measuring improvement. The playbook is the detailed schedule for execution and contains initiatives from across the opportunity spectrum.

Phase III: Execution Management and Governance

Execution Management is the process by which improvement activities are launched, executed, monitored, and communicated to everyone in the organization. We advise that organizations stick a very simple PDCA (Plan-Do-Check-Act) review format as the framework for reviewing progress, identifying problems with execution, and making adjustments accordingly to keep projects aligned to strategy. Ongoing communication is critical for keeping the strategic road map or action plan up to date.

There are two components to Execution Management:

1. Establishing accountability around key metrics

2. Developing a strong performance management infrastructure

1. Establishing Accountability around Key Metrics (via Case Teams)

Inaction that is due to the lack of clear ownership of an organization's key metrics is the number one killer of projects. Having everyone responsible but no one accountable is a recipe for doing nothing. Project execution often falls apart when a key strategic metric is controlled by peers who are all at a senior level, with none having clear authority over any of the others.

What's important is to have a single oversight of all efforts related to a given metric. We prefer a structure where that oversight is provided by **Case Teams**, groups that are each aligned with, and accountable for, one of the organization's key outcome measures. The Case Team is the holder of the strategic road map—the full project portfolio—for all levels of process improvement against the key metric (see Figure 19, next page). The purpose of this structure is to drive accountability and action.

Figure 19: Case Team Structure

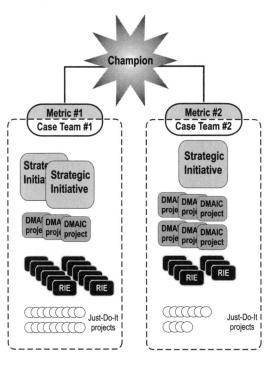

The Case Team structure organizes activities under the leadership and governance of an overall champion and key stakeholders. All projects related to a given strategic metric are assigned to a single Case Team, and it is the coming together of the multiple types of projects that moves the needle on that metric.

Since the critical outcome metric may cross functional or even organizational boundaries, a Case Team is typically made up of a single champion, three to four peer-level stakeholders, and (usually) one or two "neutral" parties who can provide fresh perspectives when settling disputes on what is best for the organization as whole.

The Case Team champion is the recognized owner of the metric in question. When ownership is blurred due to cross-functional dependencies, the champion is designated by the peer groups' superior, and his or her ownership is broadly communicated across the leadership team. Everyone must recognize that this champion is the final arbiter of decisions; there can be no confusion in this regard.

The value and importance of the champion lie in having one person clearly be the driver of action. He or she will also need to be able to resolve indecision or conflict when the Case Team members or other key stakeholders cannot agree on a path forward. This may be especially true if the necessary action would impact an outside group or have broad stakeholder implications. The champion must be able to make tough decisions that may leave others unhappy with the outcome.

The Case Team methodology avoids many common problems with implementation, ensures an orchestrated effort and a methodical level of progress, and enables quicker resolution of disputes. Finally, the Case Team is not a hands-off observer by any means. It should be thought of as a board of directors willing to get dirty as required and dive into the details to reach the right decisions and advance along the path.

Case Team Review Principles

Most of the uncertainty involved in executing a project portfolio is manageable. There *will* be unforeseen technical challenges, resource conflicts, performance issues among both the project team members and leadership, and many other problems to deal with. Having a control process that anticipates these problems, or at the very least provides alerts very early in the problem cycle, will pay big dividends in terms of overall portfolio performance. Some basic practices are outlined here:

- **Create documented project plans for all projects in the road map.** Your project road map schedule will likely have at least 40 to 50 activities that model how the work will actually be performed, the target duration, and the owners for each activity. Be sure to identify any dependencies (precedents or dependent relationships) among the activities. With the road map, you have something you can review once a week that will help to prevent surprises and improve your chances of completing projects on time.

- **Have an active control process.** Have brief update meetings weekly, and use the project schedules to highlight specific problems to solve. For instance, it is common for a specific activity to slip because a key resource gets pulled in another direction. Slips can push the overall project completion date out for days or even weeks each time and disrupt many parts of the schedule along the way. This can be prevented by updating the project schedules and addressing schedule and resource slippage weekly.

- **Engage stakeholders and sponsors actively.** Have a formal process for keeping the project team connected to sponsors and stakeholders so that progress and issues are kept visible and transparent. Sponsors and stakeholders need to know that progress is being made and when to engage in helping to solve problems.

2. Performance Management

The second major component of Execution Management is the concept of disciplined Performance Management: the infrastructure and the consistent cycle of monitoring and taking corrective action that enable leadership to make decisions based on progress against the road map execution plan.

Create a "chief of staff" for improvement

A useful model for thinking about how to manage improvement projects department-wide is the position of chief of staff in the Department of Defense. The chief of staff is often of the same rank as department heads but acts as arbitrator by virtue of reporting to the top level.

The chief of staff's peers realize that they can and should settle department-wide complexity and interdependency issues by working within the chief-of-staff forum. The alternative is to force the issue one level higher, which would make all involved appear less competent. The chief of staff is the higher authority and is relied on to make these types of tough and potentially unpopular decisions.

Applying this model to improvement efforts means appointing *one person* to oversee and manage improvement and giving that person enough authority to solve most problems and resolve most disputes. For example, Brig. Gen. Rogers was the Case Team champion for the Joint Munitions Command PVC project, responsible for seeing that related efforts moved forward and were completed on time. Similarly, John Thackrah, acting Assistant Secretary of the Navy for Research, Development and Acquisition and Deputy Assistant Secretary of the Navy for Management and Budget, was champion for several improvement initiatives, including MRAP.

Performance Management has many components, including:

a. Holding regular reviews of projects at multiple levels

b. Proactively managing the project pipeline

a. Regular reviews

Execution Management includes two distinct levels of review: short-cycle (weekly or quarterly) reviews of an individual Case Team and longer-term (semi-annual or annual) reviews of *all* the Case Teams to compare progress against strategic metrics (Figure 20).

Figure 20: Two Levels of Review

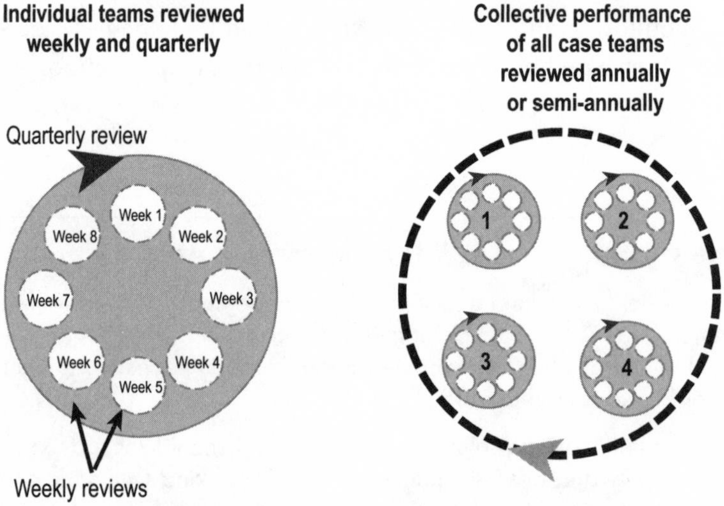

The content is essentially the same, even though the reviews happen at different levels. The appropriate level of leadership should be:

- Reviewing both outcome and effectiveness data for the projects. The data should be based on metrics that are aligned to strategic and operational priorities (see Chapter 8).

- Discussing and resolving barriers that are impeding progress.

- Gauging whether the projects are still worth the investment.

- Identifying training and support needs for the teams.

b. Proactive management of the project pipeline

Nothing in this world is static. The portfolio of projects you identify in the first go-round following an enterprise analysis needs regular review. You need to make sure that the active projects continue to represent the best possible use of your organization's resources and that there is a supply of vetted project ideas that can be launched when other projects are finished.

The senior leaders in charge of the pipeline have two crucial functions to fulfill:

- Controlling the number of active projects

- Killing projects that no longer hold promise

Controlling the number of active projects

In the parlance of Operational Excellence, we think every manager should become a fanatical supporter of the Law of Lead Time, also known as Little's Law (named after the mathematician who first proved it in 1961[2]). The law is expressed by a simple equation:

Little's Law Equation

$$\text{Average Lead Time of Any Process} = \frac{\text{Number of Things-in-Process}}{\text{Average Completion Rate}}$$

The equation applies to every process; in the context of a project portfolio you would replace "things in process" with "number of active projects."

The important aspect of Little's Law is depicted in Figure 21 (next page): **there is a simple linear relationship between the number of active projects in process and lead time.** That is, the more active projects (projects-in-process) you have, the longer it will take for *all* projects to be completed.

Figure 21: Having Too Many Active Projects Slows ALL Projects

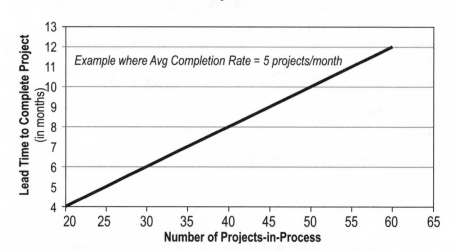

There is a simple linear relationship between the number of active projects and how long it takes to get any project done. The *more* active projects you have, the *longer* all projects will take. In the situation depicted here, the company can complete about 5 projects per month. If there are 20 active projects being worked at the same time, it will take 4 months to complete all the projects; with 50 active projects, it takes 10 months. The converse is one secret of fast project completion: the *fewer* active projects you have, the *faster* the process can flow.

In short, if you have no control over the number of projects-in-process, you we have no control over the lead time.

As some of our colleagues have discussed in other books, Little's Law applies to *all* processes, not just project pipelines. Preventing processes from becoming clogged with too much work—even if all that work is value-added from a customer's perspective—is a simple step you can take to dramatically speed up processes in your organization. (See references for details.[3])

Killing projects that no longer hold promise

There is some degree of uncertainty associated with every project. But too often, organizations feel compelled to complete every project they start, no matter what is learned along the way.

High Performance organizations, in contrast, take a "survival of the fittest" approach.

For example, New York's Metropolitan Transportation Authority, a state agency serving New York City and surrounding counties, is the Western Hemisphere's largest public transportation provider, with approximately 8.5 million riders every weekday.

The MTA had an immense pipeline of operating projects that ranged from facility improvements and software upgrades to the replacement or refurbishment of worn-out vehicles. The agency looked hard at these and other programs using a project elimination and deferral approach to prioritize its spending more effectively. Of 280 projects evaluated, 141 were identified for elimination or deferral based on the mission-driven criteria developed by the organization.

As a result, the MTA achieved savings of $40 million in 2010. Furthermore, upon completion of the project elimination initiative, the agency intends to perpetuate its savings by using the same criteria to evaluate future projects.

Restocking the pipeline

Once you begin to more actively control the type and number of projects being worked on, you'll also need to have a process in place for keeping the pipeline stocked. Think about which people or groups should have responsibility for seeing that there is always a pool of potentially high-value projects waiting in the wings to replace projects that are either completed or killed.

Keep Your Eye on the Prize

This chapter and the previous chapter have focused on making sure that any effort you expend on Operational Excellence has a payoff in terms of your bottom line, whether your measure is impact to your customer groups, stability or flexibility in your budget, reduction in costs, faster delivery of services, and so on. Creating and maintaining the links between projects and the appropriate oversight is challenging, but it becomes easier if you follow the model presented here.

As a recap:

Phase I: Identifying issues of strategic importance. Start by gaining agreement among top leadership about the strategic issues and priorities your organization is facing. Completing an enterprise analysis can help you find operational gaps or barriers—such as inefficiencies in your value streams, or the lack of policies or procedures—that are hindering your ability to address those priorities.

Phase II: Developing a balanced project portfolio. By developing project ideas around the gaps or barriers and prioritizing them based on their potential contribution to meeting the goals, you are automatically creating a pool of projects linked to the priorities.

Phase III: Execution Management. The final step is to create governance structures where responsibilities are associated with the set of projects tied to a particular strategic priority. Giving a champion and/or Case Team the responsibility for "moving the metric" is how you can maintain the link from strategy to execution.

PART II

AGILITY: RESPONSIVENESS AND INNOVATION

INTRODUCTION TO PART II

Agility is most often used to describe the ability to change direction quickly or stretch beyond usual limitations. Agility is a core element of a Performance anatomy, because there can be no "high performance" if an organization moves so slowly that it lags behind changing customer needs or cannot respond to a new demand (whether expected or unexpected).

As we'll demonstrate in **Spotlight B: Understanding Agility in the Public Sector**, the components of agility differ depending on whether you are looking at the short term or the long term. The spotlight also shows that developing the capabilities for both types of agility is necessary to establish and maintain **mission resilience**.

The remainder of this section explores steps your organization can take to develop greater agility:

- **Develop appropriate sensing mechanisms** (see Chapter 4) so that you are not stuck responding to events after the fact. Being able to detect change immediately—perhaps even anticipate or predict it—is what enables speed of action.

- **Develop innovation skills** (see Chapter 5 and Spotlight C). Incorporating innovation into your organization's anatomy is a way to expand your responsiveness. Having some basic innovation capability will help you find new ways to meet current customers' needs and to keep pace as they change. Further, innovation is critical in situations where your current systems cannot achieve the needed level of performance, no matter how much improvement you make.

History proves the cost

One of the worst examples of the dangers of rigidity was the Maginot Line, a series of concrete and steel fortifications built by the French after World War I as a defense against another German invasion. In 1940, it failed miserably.

- It was an investment in rigidity (quite literally) as a solution to what was really an agility problem.

- It was based on incorrect assumptions: that the Ardennes Forest was a barrier the German army could not cross and that technology and tactics would not change significantly over time.

- The French looked through a lens of enforced optimism and overconfidence about their solution and the size and competence of their armed forces.

- Building the structure was a huge and distracting expenditure; the attention and resources devoted to it created an organizational gravity that pulled away from alternatives.

These types of issues are as relevant to your organization today as they were to the French decades ago. Don't let your organization build new Maginot Lines, trapping you in rigid structures and practices and making you incapable of responding to changes in circumstance. Critical to any capability-building is the recognition that requirements will change and that you need the capability to respond. The consequences of failure require it.

Special thanks to Chuck McLaughlin and Mike Donnelly for help in developing the chapters in Part II.

SPOTLIGHT B

Understanding Agility in the Public Sector

The term "agility" is often used without an explanation of what it means. What would your organization look like if it were more agile than it is today? What kinds of capabilities would you have had to develop to become agile?

Agile organizations have processes and operating models that are resilient and responsive to short- and long-term demands. So the answer to those questions varies, depending on whether you're thinking about agility in the short term (responding within days or weeks to a sudden change) or the long term (anticipating changes that are coming and getting your organization prepared).

Short-Term Agility

Organizations proficient in short-term agility can be relied on by the public to respond appropriately, quickly, and effectively. Typically, they have developed the following characteristics:

- **Tactical sensing.** Having sensing mechanisms that alert you to changes that are under way. This allows you to *anticipate* where your resources will be needed most in the short term and where they would provide the most benefit to the public.

- **Pre-staged resources.** The organization positions its resources where they are needed most, allowing it to respond quickly and effectively.

- **Competency awareness.** The organization knows and understands its strengths and weaknesses. It bolsters its strengths and supplements its weaknesses with outside resources.

- **Rapid financial response.** The organization can reallocate resources and budget rapidly to meet shifting demands.

- **Flexible communications.** The organization has multiple communication channels and well-known guidelines for using communication internally and externally to support its efforts.

- **Mobility.** The organization can effectively and efficiently mobilize its resources, finances, and talent to respond to a situation.

- **Quick-change capability.** In football, the offense comes to the scrimmage line with a specific play in mind. But if the quarterback senses a change in the defense, he can call out a previously agreed-on alternate play, a **defined audible.** Every organization will face situations not covered in its strategic plans. Identifying audibles for your organization and training staff on what each means and how to respond is a good way to build agility in responding to new situations.

Short-term agility can be enhanced by incorporating Scenario Analysis (see Spotlight E in Part IV), in which the organization considers the impact of a number of different possible future events. That kind of forethought helps an organization develop a more robust playbook no matter what the future holds.

Obvious examples of public sector organizations and functions that excel in short-term agility include local fire-and-rescue units trained for rapid responses and the military's elite special forces, able to quickly deliver special, highly sensitive military operations. But short-term agility is also evident in "rapid acquisition departments" that leapfrog cumbersome procurement protocols to quickly get staff resources needed to do their jobs most effectively. The response time in crisis situations might need to be accelerated from weeks to days, hours, or mere minutes in some cases. Organizations capable of that kind of rapid respond have fostered and honed several of the traits listed above.

Long-Term Agility

While a number of organizations demonstrate agility in the short run, very few have conquered long-term agility. An organization with long-term agility has developed the following capabilities:

- **Strategic sensing.** This is the ability of an organization to anticipate changes that are further out on the horizon. Strategic sensing allows an organization to be able to take a proactive posture rather than a reactive one. Getting better at using data to anticipate trends and changes can give you a head start with this skill.

- **Robust strategic planning.** To remain agile over the long haul, an organization has to incorporate agile thinking into its strategic planning, the only activity in which most organizations formally anticipate the future. The plans should be collaborative and far-reaching, incorporating multiple scenarios of the possible future. Robust strategic planning requires a deep understanding of the organization's current strengths and opportunities and sketches out a timeline of actions for achieving strategic goals.

- **Rapid execution and operational planning capability.** Most organizations can pull off a one-time rapid response to a crisis by sheer force of will. But developing the ability to respond rapidly and repeatedly— without straining the organization to the breaking point—is a different story. The ability to respond repeatedly requires that the organization's leadership have a reliable mechanism for coming together quickly to develop action plans.

- **Adaptivity.** An organization that wants to be responsive to change cannot be glued to current practices. It must be willing to adapt, regularly evaluating how its offerings and performance compare to changing needs and making adjustments as necessary.

Public service organizations that have long-term agility can sense changes in the environment and react by changing their strategy, execution, and operating model accordingly. They don't allow short-term fires to disrupt their commitment to pursuing Operational Excellence. This single-minded commitment is a crucial discriminator between organizations that achieve High Performance and those that don't. Organizations that recognize that the Operational Excellence journey does not end when intermediate goals have been achieved will outperform others and stay relevant to citizens for the long run.

Agility and Mission Resilience

Agility is not just the ability to change what you do as circumstances change. It also includes **mission resilience**: the ability to *continue* doing what you do—fulfilling a mission and serving citizens—despite unexpected disruptive events of any scale. In fact, the capabilities associated with mission resilience are the same as those needed for agility, which is why we talk about the two issues together. To be resilient, an organization must be able to anticipate, monitor, minimize, and recover from or even prevent small and large disruptions.

Mission resilience is *not* just disaster recovery or organizational continuity plans, though they are part of the picture. One difference is that disaster-recovery capability is reactive: it doesn't kick in until after a disaster occurs. In fact, given competing priorities and limited funds, agency management may be reluctant to invest in disaster recovery capabilities it hopes never to use. In contrast, the things you do to improve mission resilience—improving communication, being clear about priorities, and so on—also improve daily mission effectiveness and are therefore beneficial even if no disaster occurs.

Your organization should focus on mission resilience (and, by implication, agility) if you can answer yes to any of the following questions:

- Does your organization face rising citizen and legislative expectations about your ability to deliver services despite disruptions?

- Does your organization have a comprehensive sensing or event-response capability that uses routine disruption responses to build skills and experience that you will need when disaster strikes?

- Have large or small disruptive events such as blizzards, transit strikes, or major delivery delays ever impaired your organization's mission-delivery capability?

- Are "routine" disruptive events (for example, power outages, seasonal flu epidemics, supply chain delays) considered part of normal operations? Do you lack a specific response plan and capability for these common disruptions?

- Have you had to analyze how routine disruptions impact your organization's quality and financial costs?

- Do external events (regulatory changes, public panics, etc.) periodically cause spikes or troughs in citizen demand for your organization's services? Would better planning and execution improve your organization's ability to respond to sudden changes in demand?

- Do you require real-time visibility into the status of cross-organizational actions undertaken to mitigate disruptions and escalations when corrective actions are delayed?

- Does accountability for responses to disruption need more clarity in your organization?

- Does your organization's disaster recovery plan focus on technology recovery rather than on full mission recovery (including people, processes, and facilities)?

- Could your organization benefit from automated response tools that would rapidly communicate status and initiate a response implementation following a high-impact disruptive event?

- Do your constituents become more dependent on your services during a disruption?

Beginning the Agility Journey

Too often, an agency's risk management approach mirrors the drawbacks of its organizational models: poorly connected functional silos, inconsistent access to information, limited management reporting tools, limited collaboration, and insufficient risk awareness across the enterprise. In recent years, many organizations have sought to correct the problem by developing more enterprise-wide (end-to-end) approaches to process management and organizational structure.

Many integrated risk management and organizational models now reflect these insights, but they still fall several steps short of a holistic, centrally guided and governed approach to maximizing agility and building mission resilience.

Such an approach should include:

- Unified presentation of data

- Real-time response capabilities

- Robust, seamless reporting across all levels

- Fully integrated access to information

- Built-in collaborative tools

- On-demand risk status and readiness assessments

The net effect of holistic resilience is a capability that reduces both the magnitude and the duration of major events. However, an agency can fully realize its mission-resilience potential only if it manages risk through the entire life cycle of mission delivery. Agencies need continuous improvement of their mission resilience efforts.

The elements listed above should give you a range of ideas for the issues you need to address if you are to develop agility. At the top of the list is improving your sensing capability, described in the next chapter.

CHAPTER 4

Knowing What's Coming Before It Happens

When Ted Egan, currently the chief economist in the San Francisco controller's office, needs a figure for sales tax revenues, he has two choices: wait six months for the state to release sales figures, or wait three days to get the latest passenger tallies from the rapid transit station nearest the Union Square shopping district. Why there? Because that district generates about 10% of the city's sales-tax revenue, and passenger tallies are a good indicator of how many people are coming to that district. Knowing the trends in passenger traffic helps Egan predict sales revenue.

Egan is among a growing number of government leaders who recognize that the best way to keep their organizations attuned to real-time conditions and prepared for the future is to identify **leading indicators** that can tell them what will be happening to the metric they're interested in, long before they can get the actual data. To build an agile, responsive organization, you can't build a management calendar if you wait until the perfect data are available. Rather, you have to be creative in looking for something you can measure *today* that tells you something useful about tomorrow. That's what a leading indicator does.

Interest in leading indicators has been on the rise for years, in part due to events that surprised the American public: *After* numerous catastrophic natural disasters wreaked havoc all across the country, we realized our emergency support services weren't equipped to quickly handle disasters of that scale, magnitude, or frequency. *After* Ponzi scheme poster-boy Bernard Madoff bilked investors of $50 billion, we realized that the existing monitoring system wasn't designed to detect that level of fraud.

In the language of High Performance, leading indicators are characterized as **sensing mechanisms** that provide early warnings of changes in the environment that would require a change in the organization. Too often, we and our governments have relied only on **lagging indicators**, signals of problems that come after the fact, when it's too late to do anything about them.

Having good sensing ability helps drive agility, efficiency, and effectiveness. The sooner you can detect a change, the sooner you can respond, and a quick response is usually more effective and less costly than a late one. Delayed responses can incur extra costs in the form of additional staff and equipment brought in to solve a problem, and even fines and penalties. Delay may also bring substantial opportunity costs—money you'll need to take away from other priorities, programs, and opportunities—if there is a long gap between the actual event and your response (see Figure 22).

Figure 22: Identifying Change Early in the Window of Opportunity

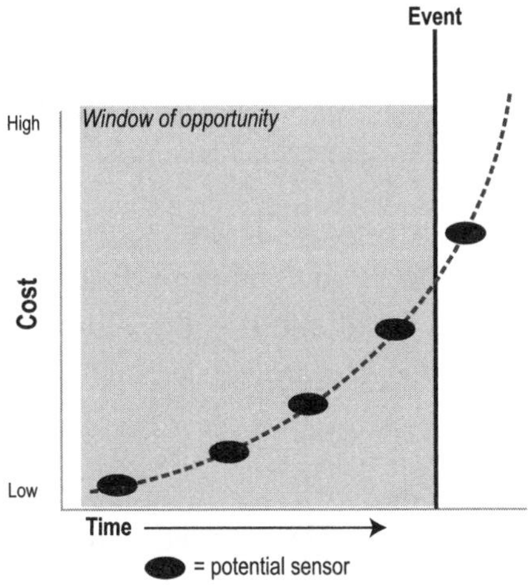

The cost of monitoring and reacting to a sensor is lower than reacting after the fact. Costs will generally be lower the earlier you can anticipate an event. Look for sensors that will give you as much warning about events as possible.

This chapter defines the importance of leading indicators and provides guidance on how you can develop your own indicators. In turn, the task of developing indicators leads you directly into the discussion of performance metrics in Chapter 8. The distinctive focus here is not on using data to monitor and continuously improve current performance but on how to develop the ability to predict what is about to happen, so you can better anticipate and prepare for the future.

Anticipate the Future with Leading Indicators

Anyone who drives a car is familiar with having dashboard instruments that monitor the car's performance. The gauges provide real-time data on what the car is doing, and good drivers monitor the data (Figure 23).

Figure 23: Dashboard with Leading Indicators

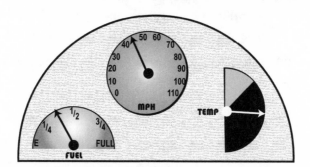

If you are a smart driver, however, you don't look at the readings just once. You look at **trends** in the data—fuel indicator dropping slowly, temperature rising, speedometer rising or falling. It is these trends and *how rapidly the readings on the gauges change* that provide leading indicators you can use to manage your "driving system."

If the fuel gauge is dropping steadily, you can predict when you'll have to stop at a gas station so you don't get stranded. If it drops suddenly, you may suspect something catastrophic like a ruptured gas tank, and you'll know that it's time for Plan B. If the temperature gauge starts to rise slowly while you're sitting at a traffic light, you know it's time to take your car in for service, before it breaks down on the highway. If it shoots up into the danger zone, you'd better pull over right away and get out of traffic.

Newer cars take warning capability even further, providing audio or visual alerts if you get too close to another car or if your speed and direction change erratically (leading indicators of potential accidents).

Now imagine for a moment that you were operating your car with only **lagging indicators** to guide you. You might not know you were speeding until you heard the police siren behind you. You would learn that the fuel tank is empty only after getting stranded alongside the highway. Clouds of steam would tell you the engine had overheated (Figure 24).

Figure 24: Dashboard of Lagging Indicators

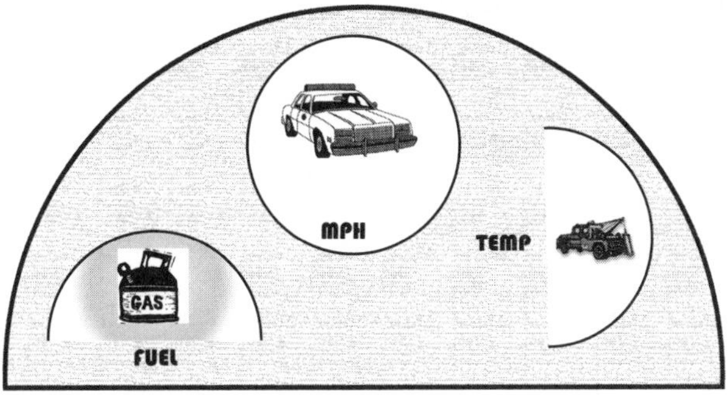

Seems absurd, doesn't it? Yet relying solely on lagging indicators is how many organizations—both public and private—are operated today. Senior leaders look only at data that tell them about the past—measurements taken after an event that tells the organization something about what just happened. The importance of a lagging indicator is its ability to confirm that a pattern is occurring or about to occur. For example, unemployment claim data are one of the most popular lagging indicators. If the unemployment rate is rising, it confirms that the economy has been doing poorly.

Leading indicators for good or bad

Keep in mind that the notion of sensing capability and leading indicators can be used for both positive and negative events. You should create indicators that will tell you of events or trends that are of benefit to your organization, as well as those that could bring potential harm or stress.

Develop Your Own Leading Indicators

Everyone on the path to building a High Performance organization encounters two challenges: (1) developing the ability to identify and use leading indicators and (2) incorporating this forward-thinking as they develop strategic agility.

As a leader in your organization, you can start by asking yourself, "How do I develop and use leading indicators in my environment?" Coming up with a good answer to a tough question requires some creativity. Let's look at two approaches and some lessons learned in other government organizations.

A Symptoms-Based Approach

The range of diagnostic tests available to a physician today is overwhelming, and it would be impractical, counterproductive, and expensive to conduct them all. Your physician narrows the list of tests by determining which leading indicators he or she needs to monitor to *predict* potential problems with your health before they cause irreparable harm. Monitoring blood sugar in a patient with a family history of diabetes, for example, is a way to monitor a symptom that is a leading indicator of potential diabetes.

The same kind of thinking can help you identify leading indicators. What symptoms could you monitor that would help you identify and predict a change in the environment (such as a shift in demands for services, a rare or unpredictable natural event) that would cause you to change something in your organization (staffing levels, funding distribution, space and resource allocation, etc.)? Identify the leading indicators, and then collect data for tracking them. Test your methods and the data itself again and again to see how accurately they help you predict the future. If the relationship turns out to be unreliable, look for a different indicator to test.

Recognize that many events share common characteristics, impacts, and, most importantly, responses. That is, there could be multiple causes of a shift in the demand for different services, but the action would be the same (shifting resources) no matter what the cause. This approach benefits from realizing, too, that response mechanisms across agencies might share similarities, meaning you may be able to create efficiencies and cost savings by developing joint responses.

For example, consider infectious diseases and transport disruptions. Both of these causes could lead to higher employee absenteeism. And both share similar responses: telework strategies, for example, are a response that would both reduce infection risk and overcome transport difficulties. Trends in absenteeism can therefore be a leading indicator to trigger an action, such as investigating the cause and perhaps implementing countermeasures that would have a positive effect, no matter what the cause of the absenteeism. We cannot know in advance when or where upheavals will occur, but we *can* develop symptom-based programs that enable quick responses regardless of the specifics.

Thinking beyond traditional data: Why the U.S. Army uses interest rates to predict enlistment

You'll probably be surprised to learn that the Army uses the spread between three specific sets of long-term and short-term interest rates to help predict enlistment. That came about because Charles Dale, Stephen D. Wilson, and Cavan Capps of the U.S. Army Research Institute found that (1) enlistment rates are closely linked to the economy, (2) the state of the economy is reflected in the demand for money, and (3) the spread between long-term and short-term interest rates is a leading indicator of money demand.

Now, the Army can look at past patterns in the spread of these interest rates to make predictions. If the economy seems to be improving (short-term interest rates are falling), enlistment will soon drop.

This example demonstrates that you may need to look beyond the borders of your agency for data that can help you predict future demands on your organization.

A Historical Approach

Imagine that you had no idea that Christmas fell on December 25th, but you did have historical data on retail sales for the past 10 years. In plotting the data, you'd find a huge spike for sales in late November through mid-December in each of those years. The regularity of the pattern would let you predict that sales this coming year would also be high in that time period. This illustrates a use of lagging data (records of past sales) as a leading indicator of future sales.

There are a lot of cautions with such uses of historical data. For one thing, this approach works only if you have an abundance of lagging indicator data and there are many months or even years of very stable trends. If the historical data shows unpredictable patterns or shifts, you can't use the data to predict what is going to happen today or tomorrow.

Also, the historical approach allows you to make predictions only within the range of how something has performed in the past. A great example is the Farmer's Almanac, which records just about every statistic relevant to farming. Farmers can use the range of recorded high and low of rainfall for their regions to make general assumptions about how to best prepare for an upcoming planting season. But Farmer's Almanac data would not help them predict a drought or heavy rains that fell outside the observed range.

Creating a leading indicator based on historical data is superficially similar to using a lagging indicator; both use the same base information. But when using historical data to create a leading indicator:

- **More information is gathered**. Data are gathered that represents more recent historical performance, not just current performance.

- **Information is analyzed for trends, patterns, and rates of change.** Analysis is performed to develop *predictions* of future trends, patterns, or shifts from the norm rather than *confirmations* of previous trends, patterns, or shifts.

- **The information is used to guide future actions.** Leading indicator data are used to trigger actions about what to do in the future, short term or long term, based on how you have performed in the past. The decision could be to push for more effort in some areas, to cut back in others, or even to abandon some efforts.

Use Multiple Indicators

In the holiday shopping example, we would be remiss if we used *only* the historical sales data to determine the projected sales. Why? Many other factors can affect sales: the overall health of the economy, consumer attitudes, spending patterns, and so on. The point is that you may need to look at multiple indicators and supplement the historical or lagging data with other experience, knowledge, facts, or insights to build an accurate forecast. That's why an agile organization looks to develop multiple indicators.

For example, in conjunction with its data warehousing and analytics work, the New York State Department of Taxation and Finance has developed a real-time selection tool that flags tax returns for prospective auditing before they are processed. The tool is built around multiple indicators, using predictive modeling to identify potentially erroneous tax credits and refunds. To date, the analytics built into the returns process function for detection of incorrect refunds and credits is credited with preventing around $250 million in incorrect refunds being paid.

Understand that indicators represent a system holistically rather than independently. Have you heard the fable about a group of blindfolded people who are asked to describe an elephant? Each gives a completely different response from the others based on what part of the elephant he or she is touching. You can't get a true image of the complete elephant unless you use *all* the data from all the people. We need to consider all our indicators together to understand what our response should be. The sum of indicators is greater than its parts.

Metrics Must Trigger Action

Christmas Day 2009 will go down in history as the day that a would-be terrorist bomber boarded a plane in London bound for New York City. What most astounded people afterwards was that every warning sign was there: he had bought the ticket for $2,831 in cash, checked no bags, left no contact information with the airline, and had been placed on a security watch list seven months prior to the attempted bombing. Even his own father had reported him as a possible threat.

In short, the *sensing* capability was present, but there was no system to trigger action based on the warning signs. Sensing capability is only as good as the actions that you take when the leading indicators or triggers are flagged.

Few people reading this book will be directly responsible for stopping terrorists, but we've all seen similar failures of early warning systems in many types of public organizations. A crucial point: the value of the information obtained from sensing capability stops at the point it is not acted on.

The purpose of having leading indicators is to **allow agile responses,** which requires that three elements work together:

1. **The leading indicators are used as triggers.** Once you have a leading indicator, the way to manage it is to establish a threshold level. When the indicator moves across the threshold (higher or lower, depending on the indicator), a response is triggered. The best time to establish thresholds is during strategic planning, so leadership can agree on what levels warrant action, and incorporate those definitions in the plan itself. Also, remember that it may be best to find ways to look at your leading indicators holistically—it may be that a response should be triggered only when several indicators hit their thresholds at the same time.

2. **Response plans are in place for multiple scenarios.** Long before the trigger is pulled, management should consider different scenarios that would cause the trigger to fire and develop appropriate response plans. Having a plan in place allows a quick response.

3. **The workforce and culture are prepared to respond.** Scenario-based response plans do not work unless the people who deliver them know what to do and how to respond appropriately at each stage of the plan. (See the discussion of defined audibles on page 75.)

The American Red Cross (ARC) is a prime example of an organization that has all three of these elements in place. It has clearly defined "disaster modes" for different levels and types of disasters, and each has its own operations manual. Each mode is associated with a trigger. For example, a house-fire trigger alerts the local fire department and initiates a call to the local ARC chapter. An impending tornado triggers a multi-county or perhaps statewide alert, and a network of affected chapters is activated to respond. If a disaster extends beyond a state's borders, a regional office coordinates the many local response efforts.

Each level and type of disaster has its own flexible, detailed, scenario-based response plan from which actions descend like falling dominoes across numerous organizations and internal departments. The plan goes into action when the trigger for that type and level of disaster is pulled.

All staff members are trained and ready to be deployed for all kinds of disasters. Everyone knows what to do in response, distinct from their regular duties, processes, and/or protocols. When the disaster-mode trigger is pulled, staff members know who's on call and who they need to work with (often different people from those they work with in daily operations). Staff members know which vendors have been pre-positioned to respond fastest and how to activate those vendor relationships. They know where and when to set up operations centers, activate pre-trained call centers, which groups to notify, and which internal groups need to be called together to make further decisions as the disaster unfolds.

Another set of triggers indicates when it's time to transition into state- and county-provided services, at which point ARC transitions out of disaster mode, back to normal operations. The triggers depend on the type of disaster, ranging from changes in weather conditions to a specific percentage decrease in the demand for services at key support sites, or call-center volumes. Throughout, the performance demands and metrics need to be flexible enough to be adjusted accordingly.

Organizations that do a good job of setting up indicators and responses can often turn a potential loss into a significant gain. Good scenario planning, threat recognition, workforce flexibility, rapid execution, and clear communication are key to creating short-term agility.

Long-Term Agility

Your agency may have planned for multiple scenarios, but how do you know if you will be sufficiently agile in the long term? What you'll need is:

- **Sustained ability for rapid execution.** As noted previously, almost any organization can respond rapidly to a disaster once. Creating the ability for rapid execution across multiple events or repeatedly throughout the years requires rigorous workforce planning and flexibility in job descriptions (so people are trained in a range of skill sets rather than just the skills needed for their everyday job). We will look at the relationships among these skill sets, and the impact on workforce and workplace culture in depth in Part IV.

- **Operational planning ability.** Knowing how the pieces of the organization must work together as a complete organism and how they interact with the environment and other organizations allows leaders to better understand what is required of the organization's workforce and culture. As discussed in Part II, leaders need to map an entire system—not just individual work units or processes—to fully appreciate what it will take to drive the outcomes they want.

- **The ability to recognize when the unexpected is about to happen.** Every organization faces unanticipated events that are not in the playbook, which means there will be no predefined response plans. To be fully agile in the long run, you need the ability to detect when something unexpected is about to happen and also to detect changes already underway in your environment that could affect your organization in the future.

Leading Indicators in a Mature Organization

Organizations that integrate leading indicators into how they manage their organization are generally more sophisticated and more mature than others when it comes to dealing with data. As you can see in Figure 25 (next page), the curve of maturity encompasses five stages.

In Stage 1 (far left of the graph), organizations are basically flying blind. Because they lack hard data, they have no idea where they are, or more important, where they are going. Organizations that want to do a better job of delivering on their mission and to outperform the competition must work on their data skills so they can move to the right along the curve.

It takes time and effort just to master the basics of data collection and analysis you need to react better to conditions in your current environment (Stages 2 and 3). Once you have that foundation in place, you can begin to develop proactive data skills (Stage 4) by working on your sensing capability, using factors such as rate of change (as discussed earlier). The key then is to continue on this trajectory and develop a monitoring and trending system to assist and guide the organization in further detection and prediction of future events.

Figure 25: Metrics Change with Improvement Maturity

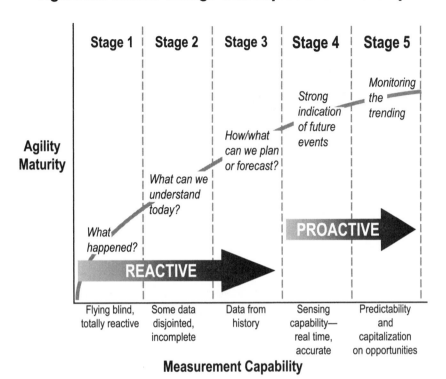

Forward-Thinking, Forward-Sensing

Which mode is more characteristic of your organization: Do you let past events direct your future? Do you manage your organization by relying solely on history and past trends? Or do you regularly use data to not only manage your processes day to day but also sense impending changes in your environment?

To become more responsive and agile in today's rapidly changing world, public sector organizations must develop a robust sensing capability based on leading indicators so that they can stay ahead of the game. The knowledge and systems needed to generate predictive data exist today, helped along by advancements in technology. We need public sector leaders who will push their organizations to develop the sensing capability that will increase their ability to forecast unforeseen events.

CHAPTER 5

The Innovation Imperative

*How (and why) to use innovation
to stay relevant and nimble*

Even if the world were a static place, striving for Operational Excellence would not be enough to keep your organization at the top of its game. Every organization has long-lasting challenges that it has never fully solved.

And as we all know, the world is not static. Challenges arise unexpectedly, missions shift as domestic and global conditions change, and resources can come and go according to public sentiment.

The ongoing welfare of your agency, the U.S. federal government, and ultimately our society depends on your ability and the ability of your public sector colleagues to adapt in the face of unprecedented social and technological change. Simply improving—doing the same things slightly better—won't be enough to keep you relevant as the world changes around you or let you keep pace with those changes. Public organizations across the board need to develop expertise in innovation.

An innovative public sector organization can expect to achieve sustainable relevance and mission accomplishment even as technology, citizen expectations, funding priorities, and social conditions in the broader environment change continuously over time.

This chapter is, first and foremost, designed to change the attitudes of anyone who thinks that innovation is either not needed or beyond the reach of his or her organization. We will also talk about fundamental concepts that will help you see real results from your innovation efforts.

Specifically, the chapter will address:

- **The meaning of "innovation."** Innovation is a slippery concept. You know it when you see it, but it is hard to describe in simple terms. Despite the difficulty in defining innovation, it helps to talk about what innovation is and isn't to help create a vision of what you're trying to achieve and how that differs from what you're doing now.

- **Challenges for innovation in the public sector.** What is and isn't unique about innovation in the public sector compared to the private sector.

- **Components of an "innovation engine."** What kinds of strategies, processes, tools, and governance you need to put in place to make innovation a more reliable source of performance improvement than it is today.

- **Leadership capacity for innovation.** Why leadership needs to take a broad view of innovation in your organization, and how that can be accomplished most effectively.

Approaching innovation as a strategically important issue for your organization and investing in developing the knowledge to do innovation correctly has big payoffs. You will be able to conduct innovation efforts more quickly and with fewer resources and achieve greater impact. Here are some typical results we see:

- Increased innovation velocity, 100–400%

- Improved initiative success rate, 20–40%

- Reduced administration costs, 40–80%

- Increased R&D productivity, 20–50%

- Increased collaboration (within and beyond the organization)

Outcomes like these demonstrate that innovation capability **can pay for itself many times over.** The emphasis throughout this chapter, therefore, is on how to generate gains in productivity and mission delivery in ways that

93

make innovation an asset for the organization rather than a drain on resources.

Understanding Innovation

Innovation can take many forms. Many people think of it as a new product or technology, but innovation can also take the form of a new service, such as online auto registration renewal. Behind the scenes, innovation can take the form of a new process or business/organizational model that enables a new way of delivering value. What does innovation really mean, then?

When *The Economist* sought to define the term innovation in a 2007 survey, the venerable magazine found that there was no universally recognized definition. It settled on "fresh thinking that creates value" as a useful working definition.

Our experience with public service organizations led us to create a slightly modified version, which borrows from the definition of Procter & Gamble chairman A. G. Lafley:

Innovation is the "conversion of new ideas into value."

Perhaps the most important aspect of this definition is that it does *not* mention "creating new ideas." That's the realm of invention, not innovation. While a degree of newness is certainly part of the nature of innovation, the novelty may be that the innovation is new to the organization, even if it is not new to the world. That is, many innovations are not entirely new but are **extensions** of existing concepts: ideas that are repurposed, adapted, or applied from another environment that is new to the organization that is adopting them.

For example, the MRAP vehicles discussed in Chapter 1 are an innovation from the U.S. military's perspective but not from the world's. They were based on designs that had been used in other countries since the 1970s. Their introduction into the U.S. military converted a "new-to-the-U.S." idea into value, contributing significantly to a 90% reduction in bomb-related fatalities.

Lafley's definition highlights two other virtues important in the public sector:

- **It emphasizes conversion.** The point of innovation is to make a difference in your ability to deliver outcomes to your customers. The best idea in the world doesn't mean much if it is never used.

- **It highlights the issue of value.** The purpose of private sector innovation is typically stated in terms of profits or financial returns associated with gaining market share or moving into entirely new markets. Those concepts have little application in the public sector, where organizations are more focused on a mission to deliver *value* in one way or another to their constituencies.[4]

For these reasons, Lafley's definition has resonated with many of our public sector clients. They find it a useful way to think about innovation.

Challenges of Innovation in the Public Sector

For the most part, innovation challenges in the public sector are remarkably similar to those faced by the private sector:

- **There is far too little of it.** Many organizations have recognized the need to invest in creating the capability for improvement and have seen continuous, incremental gains when they did so. But few devote enough resources to true innovation—finding new ways to drive leaps in performance—because their leaders either under-appreciate the value of innovation or think trying to be innovative is simply unrealistic in their environment.

- **Implementation can be frustrating.** Public sector organizations that *do* try to innovate run into common challenges:
  - Innovative ideas exist in stovepipes (with a very narrow scope) and can't get management's attention
  - Projects take too long
  - The success rate is too low
  - There aren't enough big ideas to address new needs
  - The return on the investment in innovation is too low
  - Development resources are stretched too thin

- The value of the innovation pipeline is too low (meaning the potential contribution of the ideas in the works is negligible compared to the amount of progress needed to address strategic challenges)

However, there *are* some differences in the innovation environment for public sector managers: They usually have multiple stakeholders instead of a single set of owners or supervisors; they have a mission to fulfill instead of a product or service to sell; they have fixed budgets instead of the ability to tap new markets for revenue; and they have multiple measures of success instead of a single financial standard.

Another difference between private and public sector innovation is the nature of the forces that stimulate it. In the private sector, the never-ending pressure of market competition causes firms to develop new offerings and ways of doing business. Joseph Schumpeter's "creative destruction" captures the idea of "the new" ruthlessly replacing "the old." The public sector struggles with both sides of that equation:

- **It's harder to generate the new.** Many public sector organizations highly value stability and continuity, which makes them reluctant to seek out or invest in new or untried ideas.

- **It can be nearly impossible to replace the old.** When new ideas come along in the public sector, they rarely replace the old. They just get added into the pot, increasing the clutter of activities and the competition for resources.

Also, since funding for innovation in the public sector comes from a single source (the government), market forces behave differently. As a result, government organizations can often shield themselves from the sometimes difficult processes of innovation and change.

Yet it is a mistake to think that marketlike competition does not occur in the public sector. Projects compete for funding, agencies compete for "turf," and everyone competes for a share of the taxpayer dollar. Citizens demand new services from their public servants, and eventually the government will need to deliver. Government entities that fail to keep up with demand risk a loss of relevance, as veterans of telegraph offices, horse cavalry, and wooden warships will attest.

What can you do about these challenges?

First, it's important to recognize that none of them is related to a lack of creativity or ideas. You probably have all or at least most of the ideas you need already inside your organization to become successful at innovation. The real problem is that most public sector organizations lack the knowledge, skills, systems, and will to put that creativity to good use.

What connects all these challenges is the lack of an *organizational capability* to innovate effectively. Public sector organizations on the whole have not looked at innovation strategically and asked what it would take to do it well. Few agencies or organization have agreed on when, how, and why innovation efforts will be launched; there are no systems for keeping the efforts on track; no mechanisms for supporting efforts that continue to show promise and for killing those that don't; no system for controlling the number of active projects. The result? Just look at the list of challenges—projects take too long, resources are stretched too thin, and so on.

Building a Robust Innovation Engine

To innovate in a way that helps you achieve and maintain High Performance, you have to drive consistent, repeatable innovation that generates value for customers and stakeholders. The goal is to have an enduring capability—an **innovation engine**—that will deliver innovations at the appropriate pace again and again.

The innovation engine, as shown in Figure 26 (top of next page), includes four elements:

1. **The organization's innovation strategy and mission.** This is the reason your organization exists—what would be called a "brand promise" in the private sector. This is the most important input to the engine and helps to define the mandate of the organization and how it will achieve that mandate. Achieving clarity in this step is necessary for the rest of the innovation process to proceed effectively.

2. **The end-to-end innovation process.** The process extends from generating ideas, to developing and testing new products and services, to launching the new ideas. We divide this work into three phases:

Figure 26: The Innovation Engine

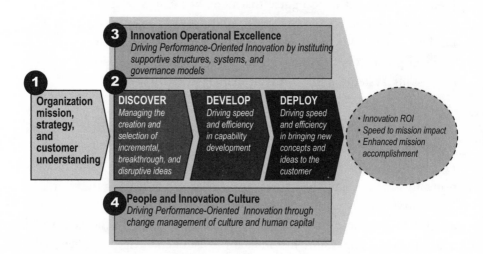

- **Discover**. The organization identifies new ideas that have the potential to be converted into value.

- **Develop**. Here, an idea becomes a meaningful concept that you can evaluate realistically. Speed is the goal in this step. You want to bring an idea to the brink of implementation quickly so you can better evaluate its potential benefits and cost and decide whether to deploy it or to kill it.

- **Deploy**. In this phase, innovation "goes live" so that customers and stakeholders can experience its value. An efficient and impressive launch and deployment plan are critical because an innovation is useless until it is deployed.

3. **Innovation Operational Excellence**. This is the **leadership capability** that connects the elements and makes sure that they all work together to deliver innovation value over time across multiple projects. Having the right governance, systems, and management processes are the focus of this element. It is the deliberate management of innovation that allows it to become a capability that contributes to High Performance rather than an unpredictable phenomenon.

4. **People management and innovation culture**. Innovation requires the right personnel policies and incentives. For instance, managers need to be rewarded for identifying and killing unpromising ideas instead

of punished for failure. A fast, efficient decision to cancel a low-value project provides a learning opportunity that is a great outcome for innovation efforts. But inappropriate policies that overemphasize taking all projects through to launch leads to wasteful spending on bad projects. The right policies and incentives, coupled with effective management of the innovation process, will over time yield a culture that supports and encourages innovation.

Each of the four elements just described is necessary to achieve Performance-oriented innovation, and it is impossible to innovate consistently and effectively without all of them. You may be able to "brute force" a single innovation project through your organization and achieve a good outcome without building an innovation engine, but you'll need all four elements to achieve consistent, repeatable innovation outcomes.

We will now focus our attention on the second and third elements: the end-to-end innovation process and Operational Excellence and the leadership capability needed to drive innovation.

(You can achieve the first element, defining your strategy and mission, through the strategic planning efforts discussed in Chapter 9. The fourth element, cultural issues, is addressed in Part III.)

The Innovation Process

One of the main lessons we emphasize for all organizations, public or private, is that innovation that takes too long is a form of institutionalized waste. If you can't complete your innovation relatively quickly, the odds are pretty good that it will be outdated by the time it's put in place.

That's why our focus in this section is on the keys to building a fast, efficient innovation process, rather than on the details of creativity. In fact, if you look at the many, many resources on innovation available in the marketplace, you'll find a lot of very good information about creativity but very little about how to make innovation fast.

The key to successful innovation is to approach the investment in innovation just as you would any other kind of investment: making sure that the return you see (the improvement in the ability to deliver on your mission) is achieved with the fastest possible speed and maximum effectiveness. Here is what speed and effectiveness mean in each phase of innovation.

Phase 1: Discover

Discovery in this context means identifying ideas that have the potential to create value for your organization. To do discovery well, you need to:

- **Identify the areas where the organization wants to innovate and where you are *not* going to innovate.** Organizational leaders are not usually well aligned in their views and may have different innovation agendas and priorities. Gaining clarity on innovation priorities will help project leaders focus efforts on areas with a potential for delivering value. For example, perhaps delivery mechanisms are in play (teams can look to new technologies to get products and services to users faster and cheaper) but not the redesign of the products or services themselves. Or perhaps you want to preserve your main value-delivery processes while reinventing core administrative functions (billing, human resources, IT, etc.).

- **Develop a deep understanding of customer needs.** As described in Spotlight A, there are many techniques for investigating customer needs. To arrive at the level of understanding needed to spark innovation, you would want to emphasize Heart of the Customer techniques, such as ethnography, which take you beyond the superficial insights gained from surveys or even interviews.

- **Become skilled at discovering and developing ideas within your organization.** There are a lot of readily available resource materials on creativity techniques. Experiment with a number of them to see what works best in your organization. Look beyond your borders by adopting an Open Innovation policy (see sidebar, next page).

Phase 2: Develop

The development stage is where organizations move from inventiveness to innovation, the creation of value. People and teams do the hard work of turning ideas into initiatives that accomplish the organization's mission in new ways. Many government organizations already have internal processes for developing innovation; some, like the Defense Advanced Research Projects Agency (DARPA), have entire departments or sister organizations devoted to research.

It's therefore likely that your group already knows the basics of turning a good idea into a viable product or service. The key to creating a true inno-

Open Innovation

Our definition of innovation means that an innovative idea has to be new to your work area but not necessarily new to your organization, your level of government, or the world at large.

In all likelihood, there are many ideas somewhere in the world that could benefit your organization. **Open Innovation** is the term applied to describe an environment where people and companies look beyond their own borders for ideas that will help them solve their challenges.

To get good at Open Innovation, develop systems and mechanisms to tap into the brainpower of people outside your organization (in sister agencies, businesses, academic institutions, research organizations, etc.) who are already tackling the problems you need to solve. The goal is to link you, the innovator with an identified problem, with solution providers.

A famous example from the private sector is Procter & Gamble's Connect & Develop program, by which the company reaches out to problem solvers outside the company to find ideas for its new growth initiatives. P&G currently receives 50% of its new product ideas from outside the company through this program.

Reaching out to others is becoming increasingly easy thanks to technology. Our company, Accenture, has a technology tool called the Accenture Collaborative Innovation Solution that allows any business or community group to collaborate with others while identifying problems, presenting and developing ideas, and creating meaningful solutions.

Accenture used this approach at a retail bank to enable managers to gather ideas from frontline employees (the people closest to customers) on how to provide new levels of service. The technology also helped employees work together to develop, evaluate, and modify these ideas—bringing the brainpower of hundreds of employees together instead of letting ideas languish inside silos.

Similar tools can help government customer-service providers use their observations and experience to put ideas into a development pipeline that can result in better satisfaction of citizen needs.

vation engine that adds more value than it expends is to make your existing processes work better and faster. In terms of developing any one innovation, the two most important efforts are (1) design and development and (2) rapid prototyping.

Design and development

The goal of design and development is to quickly turn ideas into initiatives or projects. The phase begins when an idea identified in the discovery phase is approved for further investigation. At this point, it is very likely that the idea is immature, so a top priority is to develop it to a point where a project team can work with it.

An useful approach is to develop short, focused presentations called **venture pitches** for each idea. A venture pitch—modeled on the kind of short presentation that entrepreneurs deliver to venture capitalists when seeking funding—has a prescribed format that addresses the key items senior executives need to know to decide whether to commit resources to the initiative.

The format of the venture pitch is flexible, and it can be tailored to the needs of the specific government agency. But the format should be standard for all initiatives within an agency. One proven format is:

- Idea overview (the initiative in brief)
- Potential benefits (what the initiative will bring to stakeholders and customers)
- Importance of the initiative (why the agency should undertake it)
- Business plan outline (how the initiative will be carried out):
  - Target customer or stakeholder segment
  - Funding sources
  - Required capabilities
- Potential follow-on initiatives (the next steps, if the initial idea is successful)

The venture pitch focuses the attention of the project team on the most important issues and helps supervisors quickly determine if the initiative is worthwhile.

Venture pitch development should have a tight timeline—no more than one or two weeks. Why? There will always be more research that could be done, and lax deadlines encourage staff to spend precious resources on non-essential details. Having people work quickly, using their best judgment, is a way to get sufficient detail to leadership so managers can make the call on whether a project is worth a serious investment of time, people, and funding.

The principles of "survival of the fittest" and Little's Law, discussed in Chapter 3 as part of a healthy pipeline management strategy, apply here as well.[5] Keeping a project on life support longer than necessary should be seen as a failure of project management; killing an *unpromising* project early, after reviewing it in light of the key questions, should be seen as an admirable success.

A bad outcome for a venture pitch would be to send an idea back for more research and another go/no-go decision in the future. This response indicates that the pitch did not contain the important information necessary for a decision; it is already leading to additional investment and expense for an idea that hasn't yet shown a real promise.

Rapid prototyping

As with venture pitch development, a key element of prototyping is the speed at which it is accomplished. Once the decision to move forward is made, the next focus should be on rapidly prototyping the new idea.

The prototype is what turns an airy concept into something real, whether it be a physical model or a workflow or an organization chart. It can take many forms: a process can become a pilot, a software solution can become a demo, a physical product can become a mock-up, or an organizational change can become an organization chart.

The sooner a prototype is made, regardless of how primitive, the sooner it can be tested and evaluated. Developing a prototype quickly allows for more detailed evaluation and discussion to take place, and is where life starts to stir in the new initiative.

The general idea is to work toward a complete model of the product, service, or process through a *series of rapid prototypes*, each building on the ideas that have come before. By the last test, you are essentially working from the final format, which should be ready to scale up for full deployment after capturing the lessons learned.

Phase 3: Deploy

Deploying an initiative is akin to the launch step in commerce. It gets the innovation into the hands of those who can use it to deliver value. It is the step where the promised value can become real. As in the development phase, speed is critical. Many projects get bogged down in the planning and coordination needed to support the launch of a major initiative.

Early coordination with the operations side of the agency is one key to effective deployment of an initiative. After all, once an initiative enters the normal operations of an organization, employees need to execute the initiative so that it can achieve its promise. Innovation managers and project leaders should meet early on with line leaders to coordinate how the innovation will be integrated into everyday work.

The analysis should include an understanding of training or capability gaps that must be addressed for the initiative to be successful. To avoid "analysis paralysis"—becoming locked in endless cycles of planning and analysis— learn by doing. Conduct small, low-risk tests or pilot programs to learn what does and does not work before launching it on a large scale. Follow the example of the Wright brothers, who tested their ideas on kites and in wind tunnels well before working out the details of manned flight.

Management Capability for Innovation

The first step in managing innovation is to assign a single manager or executive to oversee the entire innovation process. This seemingly obvious step does not happen in most organizations. Usually, the end-to-end innovation process, spanning from idea identification through deployment, is divided among different managers. The science and technology group focuses on research and development, another group determines requirements, and other groups will develop plans to integrate the innovation into the larger organization. The result of this disaggregation is a disjointed innovation process.

Instead, it is better to designate a senior leader as the organization's "chief innovation officer." This person may not have line-supervision responsibility over all the people who participate in innovation, but he or she should have ready access to the organization's top leaders and have responsibility for coordinating innovation activities throughout the organization. The title of this person doesn't really matter; what is critical is that the chief innovation officer have legitimate authority and the ability to evaluate and influence all parts of the innovation process.

A main concern of the chief innovation officer is to achieve the right pace and level of innovation so that it neither overwhelms the organization's capability nor generates such poor returns that it would have been better to do nothing. Those outcomes are the sole domain of management. We advise creating and managing an innovation portfolio and emphasizing strong project management.

An Innovation Portfolio

Just as you need to manage a set of improvement projects by looking at them as a whole, and you need to do the same to manage innovation projects. With a renewed focus on innovation, an organization will soon find itself with more than one initiative in the development pipeline. Innovation is always a difficult endeavor, but when managers need to oversee multiple innovation projects, the task becomes especially challenging. Inevitably, the organization will realize that it does not have the personnel or budget resources to support all the innovation projects it would like to sponsor and therefore must make tough trade-off decisions

Innovation portfolio management means more than collecting status reports on related projects. At one government client, we knew that the agency needed help in this area when a manager told us that he would "speak to the portfolio" about a particular issue. By "portfolio," he meant the heads of the project teams under his responsibility.

Innovation portfolio management involves analyzing projects along specific dimensions and making decisions to allocate resources to the initiatives that will help the organization achieve its objectives. At the simplest level, you need to plot all current innovation projects on a graph similar to the benefit-versus-effort graphs used to evaluate regular improvement projects.

For innovation projects, however, you want to compare risks versus reward—the possibility that a project will not deliver the hoped-for results (risk) against the potential that a project will help the agency deliver on its mission (reward).

When plotted this way, proposed innovation projects typically cluster in the low-risk/low-reward quadrant, perhaps with a few high-risk projects in the mix. An ideal portfolio, on the other hand, would show a grouping of projects around a 45-degree line, rising from the low-risk/low-reward corner toward the high-risk/high-reward corner. Managing the portfolio involves killing initiatives that fall outside this ideal distribution, shepherding resources and funds to projects that support it and supporting new initiatives to fill the gaps.

Effective portfolio management requires tough decisions, but it leads to cost savings by cutting bad projects, faster and more effective innovation initiatives by removing unpromising projects from the pipeline, and better delivery on the agency mission by focusing resources on projects that advance the strategy of the organization.

Project Management for Innovation

The greatest innovation principles in the world will fail to deliver value unless the work of innovation proceeds effectively. Above all, innovation project management requires rigor and discipline to ensure that the projects meet milestone reviews on time and on budget. In our experience, making this happen in the public sector requires project managers who push project teams beyond their comfort zones. Many public sector employees we've worked with place great value on their deep expertise and command of the intricate processes, regulations, facts, and histories of their organizations. These employees often display great attention to detail and live in horror of displaying a lack of knowledge about their assigned areas. However, innovation will die if it moves too slowly. So project managers have to make sure the team focuses on only the most important matters related to an initiative: What gap will the innovation fill? How will it deliver value? How can it be made to work? How will it be funded?

Getting these and other critical answers quickly—and getting those answers to decision makers at scheduled checkpoints—is the way to manage an innovation pipeline effectively. It allows decisions to be made quickly, whether to keep a project going or kill it in favor of a more promising initiative.

Making Innovation a Reality

We realize that there are issues at the polar ends of the innovation spectrum that we haven't addressed, such as establishing innovation policies in local, state, and federal agencies and how to deliver an individual, small-scale innovative solution or an individual research and development project. The former is beyond the scope of this book. But although having broader governmental endorsement of public sector innovation would certainly help, you can make progress without a national or state policy on innovation by working within the boundaries of your budget and authority. Resources on methods and approaches for delivering single projects are addressed in any number of books and courses on project management.

What we hope we have conveyed in this chapter are the benefits of devoting more attention to innovation and creating an innovation engine where policies and practices generate a string of innovations that provide demonstrable return on innovation investment. For that to happen, leadership has to play a strong role in actively managing innovation, taking an end-to-end view of the innovation process and regularly revising the portfolio of ideas to make best use of your group's resources.

The Need for Disruptive Innovation

How to stay relevant and viable in uncertain times

What products and services have you seen that you would say changed the game in the marketplace? In the past few years alone, likely candidates are smartphones and social networking sites. Products and services like these are revolutionary, changing customers' expectations about what is possible, making what came before them obsolete (or nearly so), and creating new markets.

We call these kinds of game-changing events **disruptive innovations**. They are not mere extensions of old ideas; they operate under different rules and assumptions. In their time, innovations as varied as the automobile, the fax machine, and online banking have changed the marketplace dramatically, in terms of radically lowering the costs, speed, convenience of filling a customer need, or filling needs that customers didn't know they had.

It's easy to see how valuable disruptive innovations can be in the commercial sector. Emerging companies that couldn't survive in a head-to-head competition with established market leaders create new markets in which *they* are the leader. Established companies find new customer segments they can serve in new ways to diversify their sources of revenue.

That kind of competitive pressure is absent in the public sector. But even though local, state, and federal government units are "incumbent leaders" in their domains, they need to master disruptive innovation to stay relevant and deliver on their missions. You may not have to compete for market share, but you do compete for budget, leadership attention, and relevance.

Don't see the connection between the consumer-oriented examples above and your own organization? Think of it this way: disruptive innovation is really the only option when doing what you're doing now simply won't get your organization where it needs to be. This is true even if you are making incremental gains from ongoing process improvement and innovations that don't really challenge measures of performance. You may find a need to consider disruptive innovation if:

- Your organization's mission has dramatically expanded or shifted.

- There is competition in the private sector for providing the services that your organization provides. If people have a choice, do they choose your organization? Are customers turning to another source because your services are too expensive or too complicated, or your organization is too difficult to do business with?

- Factors outside your control have radically changed the environment in which you operate. For example, your operations and budgets may have been developed under conditions that no longer hold true.

Radical changes like these occur frequently in the public sector. Table D gives some examples from both the federal and state/local levels.

Table D: Examples Where Disruptive Innovation Capability Could Help

	Federal	State/Local
Mission change	The Department of Energy's mission, originally around energy development, expanded to include nuclear weapons, then environmental cleanup and, most recently, to having a greater emphasis on energy efficiency and clean energy technology.	National Guard units, previously focused on traditional warfare and disaster relief, took on new defense and homeland security missions after 9/11.
Private sector competition	NASA has already lost some work to the private sector.	Private and charter schools compete with public schools for budget, teaching talent, and students. Home schooling also has an effect.
New constraints	Fire suppression costs now consume nearly half the U.S. Forest Service's budget, creating enormous pressure to find creative ways to perform its other functions.	Budget crises in state and local governments require rethinking of missions, priorities, and expenses.

This Spotlight highlights the differences between disruptive innovation and other kinds of innovation and improvement, and explains how those differences affect how you should lead and support disruptive innovation.

What Makes an Innovation "Disruptive"

The introduction to Part II pointed out that it helps to have an understanding of what innovation is and what it requires so you can make better decisions about where to invest your resources and determine the kinds of capabilities you really need.

Unfortunately, the definition of disruptive innovation is slippery. MIT's Gautam Mukunda has defined a disruptive innovation as one that *improves performance on a new metric but not one relevant to success of an organization's task.*

Disruptive innovations do not conform to conventional rules. While some use newly invented technology, the uniting characteristics of disruptive innovations are that they redefine the landscape in very real ways, often including one or more of the following:

- **The market served.** Disruptive innovations redefine who a customer is or could be. Southwest Airlines' original target market for its low-cost service wasn't people who already flew but people who normally used buses. In innovative communities across the country, the "market" for offender reentry programs (services for people returning to the community after serving time in jail) is no longer just the offender but also the offender's family and the community at large. Some military intelligence agencies are finding that their end users are no longer just traditional intelligence professionals focused on understanding the enemy but a much broader group of soldiers, civilians, and contractors who collaborate in developing an understanding of the threats and local populations in crisis areas.

- **The need filled/the customer expectations created.** Disruptive innovations often fill needs that customers didn't realize they had, and in doing so change expectations across the board. The convenience and ease of doing business online has created an expectation for similar capabilities in government agencies. Citizens can now fill out forms and pay taxes or parking tickets online, replacing time-consuming trips to government offices, and expect to have similar convenience when doing business with an government agency.

- **The business model embodied.** A disruptive innovation can reinvent how a private sector company makes money, or how a government organization fulfills its commitment to its customers and the public. Web-based commerce completely changed when companies like Google began earning revenue from ads rather than from purchases by users. In health care, new models are emerging for how and where care is delivered: rule-driven kiosks like the Minute Clinic at CVS stores allow nurse-practitioners to diagnose and treat a defined set of illnesses for a low fee at pharmacies and in other settings. Innovations such as these threaten to disrupt the high-cost model of the physician's office. In education, charter schools with specific missions deliver high-quality results for some targeted populations that are not as well served by one-size-fits-all public schools.

- **Measures of success.** Disruptive innovations typically "fail" if evaluated against the typical criteria of success. But they succeed in areas where traditional solutions fail. Common metrics of success applied to weapons systems in the U.S. Dept. of Defense have traditionally included being stealthy, precision guided, integrated, and cutting edge. Improvised Explosive Devices (IEDs), however, do not perform well on those dimensions. They are cheap, convenient, easy to use, and they are effective to the point where they disrupted U.S. military efforts in Iraq for years. Similarly, because they are pilotless, fly at less than supersonic speed, and lack other features associated with manned aircraft, drones (unmanned aerial systems) do not fare well when evaluated based on traditional criteria used by the Navy and Air Force. But they excel based on new measures of success because they are able to provide sustained overhead observation on targets and deliver kinetic strikes.

How to Succeed with Disruptive Innovation

The biggest factor that affects how well you manage disruptive innovation versus other kinds of innovation or improvement is the amount of knowledge you have going into the effort.

Continuous improvement and even sustaining innovations (those that work to preserve existing systems and methods) operate in what's called a **high-knowledge environment**. There is usually enough information from past experience to make reasonable assumptions to guide the change effort. For example, a team that is converting in-line processes to automated online processes can assume that the working environment will essentially be the same tomorrow as it today: the same underlying process, the same output required, the same total workload, the same people, and so on. That continuity makes it relatively easy to estimate how long the change effort will take and how much support in terms of time, resources, and dollars it will need.

In contrast, disruptive innovation happens in a **low-knowledge environment**. In some cases, it may be that *nobody* has much knowledge about what to expect. In other cases, it might be that the knowledge exists somewhere, just not in your organization. You can't know ahead of time just how a disruptive innovation will work, what capabilities it will add, what it will cost to develop, and how many resources it will take.

For that reason, most of the usual rules of project management cannot be applied to disruptive innovation. Put disruptive innovation in a head-to-head competition for resources with other projects, and it will lose every time if you use traditional measures. When working in a low-knowledge situation, you don't know what you don't know, so long-term planning or

> ## Rules that *do* apply to disruptive innovation
>
> Some rules of project management do apply to disruptive innovation, especially the need for strategic alignment and leadership clarity. As described in the previous chapter, the leadership team needs to agree on priorities and decide up front what is and what is not fair game for innovation. Disruptive innovation efforts should comprise at most between 20% and 30% of an innovation portfolio and should be considered as a means to achieve gains not possible with continuous improvement methods.

budgeting is out of the question. It simply doesn't make sense to try to develop a 2- or 3-year plan for disruptive innovation, let alone a 5- or 10-year plan. You will undoubtedly know a lot more than you do now by the time those milestones roll around, and the world may be very different in terms of customer and agency needs.

Disruptive innovators need to approach three broad areas differently from those involved in more traditional innovation efforts: approach, structure, and support for the disruptive innovation effort.[6]

Difference 1: Emergent Strategy Approach

The key to disruptive innovation is an approach alternative called **emergent strategy** or **discovery-driven planning**. This approach asks you to think of the development of a disruptive innovation as a series of experiments. Develop an idea. Test it. Learn what works. Do another test.

For example, put yourself back in time a few decades, into the mind of a personal computer developer. As you're developing this innovation, you're not sure how many people will want to buy it. You don't even know exactly what customers will use computers for.

Treating any assumptions made at the beginning of a project (development time, costs, features, etc.) as written in stone could quickly run you into a deal-killer. Hard-wired objectives, determined up front, pose another problem: by the time you complete the development, the product or service may be outdated, having been shaped for conditions that no longer exist.

Instead of focusing on the end product from the outset, pick a small piece of the puzzle. Do some development, and replace your assumptions about that piece of the puzzle with actual knowledge. Follow this path until you know enough to either kill the project or invest wholeheartedly in the ultimate outcome—either is a good decision.

Difference 2: Adjustment to Organizational Structures and Requirements

If you are going to support projects that don't operate under normal rules, you'll need to make some adjustment to how work gets done in your organization. There are two key changes:

- **Increase your knowledge of and support for advanced customer research techniques.** The best source of disruptive ideas is direct observation of the organization's customers, which is one of the most effective ways to expose unmet customer needs. Observational research about what customers are trying to accomplish and their frustrations can reveal unarticulated needs that can lead to real game-changers. Many government organizations have bureaucratic requirements-gathering processes to filter user needs and focus innovation on specific areas. These processes are fine for deliberate, sustaining innovations, but they routinely screen out unconventional ideas. Observational research can move you ahead of the usual requirements process and identify needs at the source, before they are filtered by layers of supervision and bureaucracy.

- **Shield disruptive projects from traditional pressures.** To successfully pursue disruption, the work group or department (or even agency) must be shielded from the processes and pressures of traditional organizations. The U.S. Army has shown how to build autonomous organizations dedicated to responding to disruptive threats: the Rapid Equipping Force addressed emergent warfighter needs that the traditional system had failed to meet, the IED Task Force (later, the Joint IED Defeat Organization) addressed the disruptive threat of roadside bombs and their networks, and the Asymmetric Warfare Group responded to the disruptions associated with asymmetric warfare.

Difference 3: Level and Amount of Support

Mid-level leaders play an important role in disruptive innovation because they are the most likely people to spot and propose disruptive initiatives and the most effective at building support among senior leaders. While only a civilian SES or a senior military leader can endorse the budget and development proposals, mid-level staff will most likely write the justification.

That said, the biggest demands of disruptive innovation are on senior leadership. Only senior leaders have the authority to establish and protect something that doesn't operate under normal rules. This top-level support is even more critical in the public sector than in the private sector: someone who doesn't get support for a disruptive idea in the private sector can still bring it to the marketplace by starting a new company. That option isn't available in the public sector. If you, as a public sector leader, have a disruptive idea that you think will serve your organization and its customers more effectively, your only viable option for making that idea a reality is to secure the endorsement of top-level leaders inside and likely outside your organization.

In fact, disruptive innovation requires greater direct senior leader involvement than traditional product or capability development efforts. Instead of receiving periodic briefings and reports, top leaders need to involve themselves actively in the disruptive efforts by meeting with project teams, encouraging their efforts, and removing roadblocks. The former CEO of Procter & Gamble took this active approach, as did the former vice chief of staff of the Army. Similarly, leaders of disruptive innovation efforts need ready access to top leaders so concerns can be quickly addressed.

Also, disruptive innovation efforts benefit from high levels of external input to keep the window on the world of innovation as wide as possible. Disruptive innovation leaders should dedicate a portion of their time to attending conferences, reading about innovation in the private sector or in other government organizations, engaging with consultants who can bring broad experience and professional knowledge, and exchanging ideas.

Disruptive innovators need support from human resources policies that reward, not penalize, innovation activities. Traditional measures of success are a prime example. If you were leading conventional improvement or sustaining innovation efforts, you might be held to a high standard, such as completing 75% or more of projects and generating meaningful results.

But that high of a standard simply won't work with disruptive innovation. A success rate that high would indicate a risk-averse culture that was unwilling to deliver true game-changers. A *disruptive* innovation program will, by design, have a success rate below 50%. Innovators should be rewarded when they work on "failed" projects—as long as the failure is fast and cheap and yields effective learning so that resources can be allocated elsewhere. The human resource system must value and reward disruptive innovators, even those who try again and again before delivering game-changing results.

Become a Disruptive Innovator

Again and again, disruptive innovations arise in the public sector, causing older, established models to fall. Like their commercial colleagues, government managers need to understand disruptive innovation so they can avoid being blindsided by disruptive threats and harness the power of disruptive innovation to drive new outcomes for stakeholders and customers.

With disruptive innovation, you can change your own game in ways that will help you stay (or become) relevant to the ever-changing needs of the public, increase the chances of securing funding, allow you to react more quickly to unanticipated changes, or even redesign your cost structure to enable you to maintain or expand your mission despite dwindling resources.

PART III

CULTURE AND WORKFORCE

How People Work
Will Influence *What* They Do

Some years ago, the flight crew for a C-130 military cargo plane was told that its base was going to embrace "teamwork." It sounded good, until the crew members were told that any team meetings would have to be held on personal time. Later, the crew saw that none of their recommendations was being supported by their superior officer. Not surprisingly, "teamwork" had a very short shelf life at that base.

It's clear that the base leadership was just paying lip service to ideas of teamwork and collaboration at that time. The leaders made no changes in policies or practices—or in their own behavior—to support their stated goal. Experiences like this demonstrate why leaders in High Performance organizations must change their culture, policies, and leadership practices in ways that enable work on Operational Excellence and agility:

- Thinking through what decisions can be made at what level, moving accountability down to lower levels wherever possible

- Promoting regular use of communication processes and practices to ensure that employees are aware of their work unit's goals, policies, current performance, and gaps and how those align with and contribute to mission success

- Gathering data regularly, organizing and making the data accessible to everyone involved in a decision

- Rewarding and supporting collaboration

- Seeing to it that culture and values are understood, maintained, and woven into the fabric of workforce performance

- Reinforcing new norms consistently

You will have to deal with a lot of issues to create an organization in which culture and norms enhance your ability to achieve higher performance. The places to start are:

- Focus on what your leadership does (Chapter 6)
- Identify the biggest gaps in the skill sets of your employees (Chapter 7)
- Establish a new measurement system that is consistent with your strategic goals (Chapter 8)
- Make sure you manage a change, not just react to it (Spotlight D)

Special thanks to Breck Marshall and William Gripman for help in developing the chapters in Part III.

CHAPTER 6

Leadership to Galvanize Your Workforce

We presume that you're reading this book because, like us, you believe that a radical transformation of performance in our governments is imperative and that major changes are needed in how public sector organizations operate. Universally, the single best predictor of success or failure to generate High Performance is the degree to which leadership at all levels is engaged—not just tolerating new procedures and standards or even by being verbally supportive but actively promoting, guiding, and working continuously to improve how work is done.

To create an organizational anatomy capable of achieving High Performance consistently, your organization's leadership has to be a visible agent for change and publicly demonstrate its commitment. Most critically, leaders need to provide strategic direction, be proactive in aligning stakeholders across the organization, remove barriers, and make changes in their own and the organization's practices. In a memorandum, U.S. Secretary of the Navy Donald C. Winter put it this way:

> In addition to being engaged in combat operations, the Navy and Marines are transforming to meet future challenges. I value leaders who can be change agents. . . . I also value leaders who can successfully cascade this higher level guidance into the goals of their lower-echelon organization.

In this chapter, we'll look at how leadership relates to building a Performance anatomy.

Change Requires Leadership, Not Just Management

The terms *leadership* and *management* are often used synonymously, both associated with words like supervision, administration, and command. We take a different view, making a clear distinction between the two (see Table E). Management comprises the functions needed to get work done day to day, such as planning, organizing, staffing, and controlling an organization or effort for the purpose of accomplishing a goal. Leadership is about setting agendas, not just reacting to them, identifying priority issues and problems for an organization or work group, and initiating change that leads to substantive improvement.

Table E: Managers versus Leaders[7]

Managers	Leaders
• Organize and direct the present and near future	• Inspire others to deliver superior performance
• Focus on efficiency	• Persuade others to change
• Find answers and solutions	• Serve as agents for growth and development of others
• Create policies to implement principles and standards	• Formulate questions and standards
• Ground decisions in data	• Focus on outcomes and effectiveness
• Track and oversee transactions	• Deal with uncertainty and ambiguity
	• Develop the organization that is yet to happen

Think about the kinds of changes described in previous chapters of this book. Achieving the kind of alignment required to drive meaningful and measurable results from Operational Excellence requires that everyone in the organization be clear about priorities and consistent in striving toward new metrics of success. Similarly, agility requires new practices that encourage and reward the anticipation of future events and innovation instead of stifling them. Only leaders have the broader span of authority and responsibility to establish and enforce a new vision, to make sure that departmental or unit managers think beyond their small spheres of influence, and to make sure that barriers to consistency across the organization are removed.

Public sector leaders who have made or are currently making the transformation from old ways of operating to the new paradigms uniformly say they came to a personal epiphany: if they were really serious about making a major shift in the outcomes their organization could achieve, it would take dedication and commitment and a lot of energy from them personally.

What Performance-Oriented Leaders Think and Do

Research by some of our Accenture colleagues revealed eight behaviors associated with people considered to be "best leaders."[8] We clustered them into three categories and realized that these behaviors correspond to the kinds of questions that Performance-oriented leaders ask themselves.

Category 1: What Is the End I'm Trying to Achieve?

Leaders who succeed in creating High Performance organizations are keenly aware of the need to establish a clear vision of where they want to go and their role in making it happen. They ask themselves questions such as:

- What is important to me and to the organization?
- What should we try to accomplish?
- Is it time for someone to get things moving?

To answer those questions they engage in the first three behaviors that arose in our research:

1. Clarify personal values, purpose, and objectives.
2. Work with other leaders to establish the organization's mission, vision, strategy, and goals.
3. Take initiative and responsibility for leadership.

Category 2: What Will It Take to Get There?

Both good leaders and great leaders know that they have to communicate their organization's vision, mission, and goals. But great leaders take it one step further: they look at what it will take in practice to push the mission down into every level of the organization and also at what needs to be reported back up to best monitor progress.

After Performance-oriented leaders have figured out where they and their organization are going, they next need to determine what it will take to get there. They ask themselves question such as:

- What kind of operating model will help us? Where does our current operating model fall short or stand in the way of working in the new way?

- How should we organize this effort?

- How can we get work done most efficiently?

- What are the tough choices I face?

Being a leader whom others will follow

The Accenture researchers who produced our report on Performance-oriented leadership, Richard A. Hagberg and Yaarit Silverstone, also say that what makes a leader someone whom others are willing to follow is the way the leader shows up. "Their daily performance in the workplace exemplifies the attitudes and behaviors they desire from [others]. They demonstrate energy, tireless commitment, hard work and determination to success—but also strategic thinking that focuses action into the most useful channels. They are positive and optimistic even in difficult times, enthusiastic about the organization's projects and goals, eternally sanguine about achieving desired results."

In short, what makes someone want to follow another person is the leader's positive, can-do attitude and behavior, and ability to remain calm and confident even when faced with setbacks and project or organization problems.

When it comes to creating change of the types discussed in this book, there is another critical element: **credibility**. You have to get involved personally so you can speak to your organization in the first person: "This is what I've done. This is what I learned about why this is important to our organization. Here's how it worked for me. Here's what will work for us."

Finding the answers to those questions leads to the next three behaviors that distinguish the best leaders:

4. They design an organization structure and develop or re-engineer systems and processes for the operating model.

5. They take a fact-based approach to making decisions.

6. They monitor actions and events and achieve follow-through.

Category 3: Rallying the Resources

As the mission and mechanisms are being worked out, Performance-oriented leaders are also thinking about how they can engage employees in making the changes happen. Typical questions include:

- Who can help me to get there?

- How can I get their support?

- How do I get synergy from a group of individuals?

Answering these questions leads to the last two of the top eight behaviors observed in Performance-oriented leaders:

7. They recruit and build a team.

8. They persuade others to join the effort.

Eight Lessons from Public Sector Leaders

Our experience across numerous private sector and government organizations has led to one firm conclusion: leaders who do not practice the principles of Operational Excellence or agility themselves cannot lead a transformation to High Performance.

We have run across leaders who willingly sign up their organization, kick off programs and initiatives, and then disappear while the subordinates do all the heavy lifting. No wonder the efforts ultimately fail to generate the results everyone is hoping for.

That's why, in addition to the broad lessons about Performance-oriented leadership, we present some recommendations given to us by public sector leaders who told us what enabled their leadership teams to work together effectively in driving new norms and obtaining improved results.

1. Think about "Mission Cost"

One of the biggest shifts in thinking that must occur is captured in our definition of higher productivity: more mission at equal or lower cost. Costs have always been front and center in private sector decisions. In the public sector "budget execution" is the mind-set, a theme captured succinctly by Vice Adm. Walter B. Massenburg when he was a commander in the Naval Air Systems Command

> We had three depots and in essence their incentive was totally misaligned with the fleet. They chased dollars at all costs, production at no consequence. And when pressured with budget cuts, they normally reverted to reduction in force. . . . When I became the Depot Commander, I became more focused on what we VAL-UED. And the value set was government depot capability, that valued Sailors and Marines. The goals we set, the priorities, were reliability increases and cycle time reduction. . . . The metric for our "main thing" was readiness, which matured into "readiness at cost."

This blending of cost considerations into mission delivery deliberations is a welcome addition in many public sector circles. An SES in a financial office recalled for us, "When I was in the private sector, if my organization didn't stay in the black for two quarters. . . . I'd get shut down around the third quarter. [My bosses] would tell me I hadn't struck any oil yet so I was likely drilling a dry hole, and it was time to put the company's money elsewhere."

Tip: Reengineer your leadership meetings

Part of reengineering systems and processes to better support a Performance anatomy should include restructuring leadership meetings so that mission and strategy are reviewed regularly, along with evaluating whether work being done on priorities is making measurable progress. List your top goals on all agendas and review new issues in the context of those priorities.

What the financial officer liked about the private sector was that he always had a sense of urgency around delivering results. He says that public sector leaders should do the same, with the focus shifted from "financial results" to "mission results"—what is being delivered for the resource investment.

2. Think about Your Sphere of Influence

Mid-level public sector management and sometimes even with senior management often think they don't have enough control over anything to embrace the kinds of changes required for High Performance. They point to regulations or complexity as the main culprit.

However, other leaders have said they've been amazed at how much progress they can make just within their own sphere of influence. "It may take time to deal with changes to regulations at a strategic level," one leader told us, "but there are a lot of other things you can work on [around productivity and agility] within what you *can* control. When you start doing value stream mapping . . . [you find] a tremendous number of internal impediments that you do control and can improve."

A second approach is to use mechanisms that bring different offices, departments, or agencies together, so that leadership representing all the pieces of puzzle can develop shared priorities and understanding. Enterprise analysis is one such mechanism (see Ch. 2).

3. Fight the Fears

In the past, a call to "increase productivity" or "cut costs" has often been a justification for what is euphemistically called "workforce reductions." When you announce that your organization is embarking on efforts to improve performance, you can anticipate that some people will interpret that as a warning that job cuts are to come.

And that's not the only source of fear. As outlined in previous chapters, the foundation of a transformation effort is an honest look at where you are today and what you need to do tomorrow. De facto, you will be defining changes that need to occur. You will have to question *why* and *how* tasks are currently being done and decisions being made—an examination that will naturally make people feel defensive.

Is the intent to streamline processes and reduce staff hours? Absolutely. Is it to then get rid of people? Absolutely not. By a large margin, the public sector organizations we've worked with have much more demand for services than they can currently handle. We commonly hear the complaint that, "There are areas we're not touching right now because we don't have the manpower."

The purpose of productivity improvements is twofold: to position the organization to be able to respond to more of the current demand and to give you some elbow room to be more agile in responding to shifting or unanticipated demands in the future.

4. Experience Operational Excellence Firsthand

A general at MedCom, the U.S. Army's medical division, who was about to lead a major push toward Operational Excellence told us that in preparation he visited a large medical corporation that had been involved in quality improvement for several years. The CEO of that company had invited other industry leaders to also share their experiences and arranged to have several project teams make presentations.

This kind of exposure led to insights far beyond the kind of learning that can happen through reading or attending workshops. Not only did the general learn a lot about how to make improvement happen in a large organization, but he also got a lesson in the infectious enthusiasm that can result. He said the project teams he saw "were describing how they'd been going home day after day, year after year, frustrated with the way that they were doing things. And finally somebody asked them to be on this [improvement team] and it transformed the way they looked at everything they did."

5. Learn by Doing

One of the tenets of adult learning is based on the saying, "Education creates understanding, but only practice creates belief." In anything we have learned to do well in life, practical application and success change what we believe is possible. So to truly change the way an organization does business—a DNA-level change—leaders have to experience the execution and benefits of Operational Excellence and agility personally. Only then will they become convinced of the possibilities and begin using the methods in their day-to-day business.

6. Empower Teams in Decision Making

A number of public sector leaders who have adopted new approaches have admitted to us that their old gatekeeper mentality, their command-and-control style of leadership, served mostly to slow down the speed of decision making and action—without adding to the value delivered to customers. Speed is a critical ingredient of High Performance, so leaders need to make sure that their workforce is properly educated in the goals and values of their organization so the leaders will feel more comfortable delegating decision-making authority and responsibility appropriately to accomplish more in less time.

7. Become More Accessible

Tomorrow's government leaders need to be more accessible to key constituents and the rest of the leadership base. They should allow for collaboration and foster an atmosphere of teamwork and success. Given the more virtual and open style of today's and tomorrow's workplace environments, they need to master operating transparently in person and in multiple media.

8. Become a Communications Beacon

The single most important factor in leading change is communication. Staff members in your organization should come to see you as a communications beacon: The person who keeps them abreast of leadership's decisions about directions and priorities. The person who clearly communicates what changes are coming down the pike, why those changes are important, and what will be done to help employees adapt to the changes. The person who shares information openly with employees who need that information to do their jobs effectively.

By becoming a communications beacon, you become the person who helps employees stay on track, better able to keep their work aligned with the organization's priorities. You become a valuable asset and someone they will trust to lead them in the right direction.

Determining Leadership Development Needs

Since leadership plays such a critical role in creating the kinds of changes we're talking about in this book, one key step is making sure that people in leadership positions have the opportunity to develop the knowledge and skills needed to develop a strong Performance anatomy. That need is particularly important in the public sector, for a number of reasons:

- Success with both Operational Excellence and agility requires knowledge of business practices that are quite common in the private sector but are only now gaining a foothold in the public sector. These range from cost-wise accounting to conducting management reviews of improvement efforts.

- Senior leaders in the public sector don't have the same flexibility in hiring and firing as do their private sector counterparts. They have to work harder to win over people who might be reluctant to participate in change of any kind, especially those who have developed a mentality of "waiting out" changes. Educating the leadership levels and making sure they are actively involved so that they can see the benefits for themselves are critical elements.

- Because of the relatively high rate of turnover at leadership levels throughout the military and at the higher levels of civilian agencies, you will be able to create sustained change only if you can reach the middle and senior levels. As one military commander told us:

  > My real audience has to be a level down from [the generals] because those are the people who will execute the program day to day and will graduate up into those senior leadership positions. I have to win them over if I'm going to succeed in the long term because they are the ones that will perpetuate this and sustain it long enough . . . to get the results and [see the] cultural change."

  A captain in the U.S. Coast Guard expressed a similar sentiment: "So far, I consider my best achievement to be laying the foundation for my people. . . . I spent my first three months talking to the division chiefs about process improvement and process agility and addressing it in internal newsletters."

129

Does your organization have a need to develop its leaders? An organization should answer critical questions in regard to leadership issues and challenges to determine the need for leadership development (Table F).

Table F: Leadership Development Questions

Are individual leaders effective?	• Do individuals on the leadership team focus on the current business or are they looking out to the future? • Are individuals on the leadership team providing clear direction and focus in driving the organization toward its vision? • Do all individuals present a united front with regard to the vision? • Have change initiatives been successful?
Are leadership teams effective?	• Are leadership teams aligned to the strategic direction of the organization? • Is there good and frequent communication between all members? • Is there a good sense of team spirit? • Are leadership team members willing to challenge each other's viewpoints?
Are leadership processes effective?	• Does the leadership team understand who takes responsibility for setting strategic direction, managing stakeholder relationships, developing the organizations, managing business performance, aligning the organization to strategic direction, and managing change? • Can the organization implement these processes at pace so it can take advantage of opportunities? • Does the team effectively communicate performance strategy across the organization? • Are the appropriate individuals empowered to make effective decisions?
Is the organization growing future leaders?	• Does the organization identify and develop its outstanding performers so they are ready for key executive positions? • Is it clear where future leaders of the organization will come from? • Does the organization have a career development program? • Are senior executives experienced at leading change?

Making Sure Your Leaders Lead

Time and again, we've seen implementations falter because of a lack of leadership involvement. In fact, it's not just involvement you need but full engagement of top leaders. If you want a ghost of a chance at creating a new anatomy, one capable of sustained higher performance, your leaders must be actively spearheading the effort, practicing the new behaviors themselves, and holding employees accountable for doing the same.

CHAPTER 7

Ready, Willing, and Able

Creating the capability for Operational Excellence and agility

Imagine your workplace 5 or 10 years from now. You have been successful at driving down costs, improving productivity, and expanding your ability to serve your customers and your mission. You respond to ever-changing demands with an envied nimbleness.

Now imagine transporting your workforce of today to that organization of the future. Would they have the skills and knowledge to fulfill the new demands? Would they have incentives to embrace the changes, or would the current ways of doing business stand in the way?

In recent decades, thousands of organizations in the public and private sector have launched "transformation" efforts. Many achieved impressive gains only to see progress erode away because their organization's culture and norms remained firmly rooted in traditions of the past. If you want new and better outcomes—whether doing more of what you already do (faster and cheaper) or becoming proficient at meeting new demands—your employees cannot continue to do exactly what they do today, no matter how good they are.

To get the most out of your Operational Excellence and agility efforts, you need a highly engaged, skilled, and productive workforce: the right people with the right skills, doing the right things to contribute to the long-term success of the organization. In this chapter, we'll talk about how to decide what this means for your organization in the context of creating the right anatomy for higher performance.

The Three Components of Capability

We use a simple model to help managers think through workforce development issues. The three components of capability can be simplified into three terms: ready, willing, and able (see Figure 27).

Figure 27: Ready, Willing, and Able

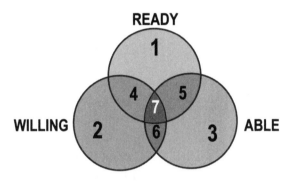

Ready (Zone 1): The workforce is prepared to act to meet any and all workplace demands; employees have the resources they need, know what is expected, and are aligned with strategy

Willing (Zone 2): The workforce is aware of the need to abandon old practices, to commit to adopting new practices as required, and to understand that new incentives provide the motivation for change; leaders have removed any barriers to change

Able (Zone 3): The workforce has the tools, skills, knowledge, experience, and judgment required to do the required work

The sweet spot (Zone 7 in the diagram) is where all three components overlap; that is where you achieve true capability. A key message behind this figure is that it takes *all three elements* to achieve Operational Excellence and agility. If you ignore any of them, your efforts will ultimately flounder.

Ready, willing, but *not able* (Zone 4): You have a workforce that *wants* to change and even has the incentives to do so, but it does not have

133

the required skills. Think about all the medical clinics in the winter of 2009–2010 that were ready and willing to administer swine flu vaccine but were unable to do so for months because of production limitations.

Ready, able, but *not willing* **(Zone 5):** The workforce has the skills and resources, but the conditions do not exist inside the organization to make people want to try something new. Remember the C-130 flight crew referred to in the introduction of this section? That crew was ready to adopt team behavior and even able to do so. But after seeing that base leadership did not support the change, the crew members soon became unwilling to do so. Employees in many public sector organizations are frustrated by a similar situation: they would like to change, but old policies or practices stand in the way.

Willing, able, but *not ready* **(Zone 6):** Incentives and motivation? Check! Skills and knowledge? Check! Resources for doing work in new ways? Um … not so fast. A prime example of a Zone 6 situation was FEMA's response after Hurricane Katrina. Many organizations wanted to help and had the knowledge and capability to do so, but the agency lacked a comprehensive "approach to managing the development of emergency preparedness policies and plans."[9] Since then, FEMA has made several changes, including the adoption of a National Response Framework and three private sector standards for use by U.S. companies in emergency planning and response.

As you look out to the future, whether that be next month or five years from now, the questions you have to answer are *what has to change* and *in what*

Workforce as a leadership issue

While this chapter focuses on workforce issues, at its core it is as much about leadership as was the previous chapter. Only leaders have the ability to create the *organizational conditions* that will allow *individuals* to embrace new methods, new knowledge, and new policies. So our focus here is not on specific kinds of training or opportunities that any single person needs to become proficient in Operational Excellence or agility. Rather, we look at the kinds of decisions that leaders must make to create an entire workforce that supports those goals.

ways so your workforce will be ready, willing, and able—capable—of the kind of performance you want to create? What will it take to create a workforce that is good at process analysis, strategic linkage, data-based improvement, sensing, and innovation? What will you have to change so that your organization continually discovers and implements new efficiencies, delivers more of what your customers want, and responds quickly to change?

As pointed out in the previous sections of this book, the world is not a static place, so you have to ask all these questions regularly and continue to adjust what you're doing at each stage to stay relevant in the future.

The Cost of Un-capability

Anxiety over poor mission capability and the costs that poor capability can exact is especially burdensome for those in public service. An unfortunate consequence of funding, budgeting, and accounting mechanisms is that the total costs of poor mission capability are rarely recognized. Yet the costs are often very high, usually paid downstream (by the people at the end of the line), and in many instances preventable.

In short, while the cost of unreadiness is not readily visible on a taxpayer's bill, it is paid in many ways, as shown in Figure 28.

Figure 28: Cost of Poor Mission Capability

	Unready	Unable	Unwilling
Customer	• Unmet threats • Mission shortfalls	• Lose public confidence	• Loss of funding
Process	• Delays • Loss • Inventory	• Recovery • Repair	• Misalignment • Increased complexity
Culture	• Risk averse • Overcompensation	• Added oversight	• Misdirection • Silos

Long-term impact	Short-term impact
• Diminished capacity • Precipitate downstream damage	• Non-value-added activities • Generate waste

The consequences of poor capability in public service have an often immeasurable flow downward in terms of societal costs and consequences. Crime statistics in Houston, Texas, rose in the wake of Katrina, an aftershock of mass migration into that community.

Strengthening Mission Capability

How do you make sure your organization has achieved the sweet spot, the overlap of Ready, Willing, and Able? Here are a few ideas to get you started.

Getting Ready

Preparing a workforce for Operational Excellence and agility means providing the knowledge and skills needed for improvement and innovation and creating the capacity to rapidly add skills or retool existing skills of the workforce as circumstances change. A workforce can be ready for High Performance only if there is a supportive environment based on collaboration.

One of the most important ingredients is how knowledge and information are treated. High Performance organizations do not restrict the flow of information or treat knowledge as a scarce resource that only a privileged few get to use. Effective knowledge sharing is planned and measured, leading to higher productivity, greater engagement, and broader capabilities. To make it happen, you will need to address five elements:

1. **Strategy**: Establish a robust knowledge management approach that aligns with and supports the organization's mission and capabilities

2. **People**: Establish effective ways of working that promote collaboration among key people; tap into the knowledge of high-performing team members; promote the sharing of knowledge and expertise

3. **Process**: Set up processes that reinforce knowledge sharing and knowledge transfer

4. **Technology**: Implement tools that enable collaboration and knowledge sharing

5. **Evaluation**: Create metrics around knowledge sharing; use them to communicate the benefits achieved through knowledge transfer

Provide the workforce with an optimal blend of learning and communication, ranging from formal classroom training and informal on-the-job learning to social networking, online collaboration, and software applications that provide simulations, virtual worlds, and games. The more efficiently employees can tap into each other's expertise, the more effectively organizations can respond to the needs of clients. Facilitating knowledge sharing within the organization means using proactive approaches for knowledge transfer and knowledge sharing, such as building knowledge repositories and holding knowledge-sharing sessions and workshops. It also means being open to exploring emerging, innovative options for facilitating open collaboration.

These changes are much easier said than done. As you may have already experienced, moving to a collaborative learning environment is often a tremendous cultural shift for many organizations. Leaders have to be persistent in driving the cultural change.

Eliminating Barriers to Willingness

Universally, the people we've worked with in the public sector *want* to do the right thing. They want to provide good service. They want to deliver on their organization's mission. The internal motivation for *doing the right things better* is unsurpassed. But that desire to do good has not always translated into a willingness to adopt change. Why? You need to look at policies and practices in your organization that make people afraid to try new things.

For example, do you reward people for eliminating waste? For participating on improvement teams? For innovation? Have you taken steps to help people adapt to a more rapid pace of change?

Odds are good that if you look at your organization's incentives, you'll discover *dis*incentives for transformation. Policies may reflect bygone values that are absolutely wrong for transformation today.

You need to get your leadership to define what it is you value today—in terms of mission outcomes, teamwork, innovation, fiscal responsibility, and other factors—and make sure that any policies, incentives, and metrics reinforce those values.

When Vice Adm. Walter Massenburg became a depot commander, for example, his team realized that it wanted incentives and metrics that reflected priorities centered on increasing reliability and reducing cycle times for service to sailors and marines. The next chapter includes more information on identifying and applying metrics.

Look at the full range of motivators

Motivations that lead people to learn new skills and embrace changes like data-based improvement or innovation are a subset of employee motivators in general. For example, it is extremely unlikely that people will be motivated to adopt quality improvement practices if they are not also highly motivated to support the work of your organization.

Motivated employees tend to be high performers who are engaged in their jobs. A highly motivated workforce often benefits from increased productivity, higher job satisfaction, higher engagement, reduced absenteeism, lower turnover, and increased identification with the organization's values and mission. Therefore, as you consider ways to create a culture capable of higher performance levels, look at the broader context of employee motivation in your organization.

Factors aside from financial compensation motivate employees and are as varied as the workforces of today. Creating a culture of trust, leveraging the power of peer recognition, and focusing on the enablers and tools that help people reach their potential in an increasingly complex business environment are all critical components of motivating organizational workforces. By gaining a deeper knowledge of human motivation, you can put in place a more holistic approach—one that integrates people, process, technology, and compensation strategies that encourage and reward the behaviors that produce High Performance.

Making Sure Your Workforce Is Able

Rear Adm. W. Mark Skinner, former commander of the Naval Air Warfare Center Weapons Division at China Lake and Point Mugu, California, once told us:

> People walk through the gate at China Lake every day and want to do a good job. But in the new environment we are in, where resources are shrinking—be it people or money—it's not enough to do a good job. We have to do it better every day.

Suppose you were the supervisor of a key service area in your organization. One day, upper management tells you that you are to lead an improvement project to cut delivery time by 25% within two months. You've never done anything like this before. What skills or knowledge would you need to have a reasonable chance of success? At the top of the list is how to be an effective team leader: getting people involved, using everyone's knowledge, running meetings that aren't a waste of time. Right after that might come skills in using data and formal problem-solving methods, knowledge of how to document results in a way that is useful for the organization, and insights in balancing the need for collaboration with the need for speed.

Now suppose the challenge was to completely redesign the service so the goals could be met in less than half the time with half the resources, while improving the results for the customer. Small, incremental improvements won't do the trick, so you'd need all the skills listed above; plus it would be helpful to know something about innovation and creativity.

These two scenarios are just the tip of the iceberg in terms of skills and knowledge that your workforce of the future will need. Technological changes alone are going to require rapid re-skilling in both the near and distant future. There are a great number of tools, methods, and skills required for success at Operational Excellence and agility. You need to develop a plan for teaching skills to your workforce, either hiring people who can teach them or contracting with third-party experts, as needed.

From Good to Best

No matter what scenario you envision, government organizations in the future will have to function differently.

If you prepare people for the changes—give them the resources, skills, and incentives—magic occurs. People feel in more control of their own work, their own processes, and their destinies. They get excited about buying into the changes because it makes their work lives easier and more rewarding. When that happens it is much easier to get buy-in, because people see good results for themselves and taxpayers.

CHAPTER 8

What Gets Measured Gets Done

Before being promoted to head a large, complex military organization, a U.S. Army general was in charge of a smaller subordinate command. In that position, he was charged with executing the day-to-day base services. He well understood the challenge of having to execute the business and still be responsive to his stakeholders at headquarters. He recalls being constantly aware of the tension set up by the metrics his command was supposed to meet. A number of metrics stressed efficiency but none focused on effectiveness. For example, to meet its metrics, his command only had to do its work faster and with minimal resources, whether or not the services met the customer requirements!

This kind of disconnect is quite common in the public sector because little attention has been paid to the importance of metrics. We've seen organizations under pressure by leadership to operate only 5 days a week while at the same time being asked by customers to make their service available 7 days a week (so the customers can meet *their* mission requirements).

Incomplete, unbalanced, or competing metrics create chaos in an organization. Everyone will do the work that he or she is to be measured on, in a way that will make that metric look as good as possible. But if we are measured only on efficiency, that's what we're going to focus on, whether or not it helps our organization fulfill its mission to its customers and stakeholders.

In this book, we talk about creating new structures, practices, and policies inside your organization to enable you to achieve higher levels of performance. As you clarify what that means for your organization, updating your system of metrics will be critical to drive and maintain the changes you want to see. The role of metrics in supporting the goals of a Performance anatomy are summarized in Table G.

Table G. Metrics for a Performance Anatomy

Purpose	How metrics help achieve that purpose
Align all components of your performance improvement effort (people, processes, technology, infrastructure)	• Help align stakeholder interests with achieving a set of target business benefits • Provide a basis for deciding key issues • Facilitate a consensus on what is important about how the organization works
Make progress on issues important to the organization and its customers and stakeholders	• Force discussions about what is important to the organization • Provide an accurate reflection of performance that allows leaders to make better decisions about where goals are and are not being met
Adapt to the fast pace of organizational change	• Provide valuable insights into deviations from the business plan and help to identify bottlenecks; these insights can help accelerate delivery of value across both strategic and tactical projects • Identify root causes of problems affecting business operations
Drive ongoing improvement and change	• Show past patterns and projections of familiar metrics that can help leadership explain the impact on the organization when changes are planned or undertaken • Provide the capability to identify which processes or areas to address or bring into focus, thus supporting better investment of resources
Provide a consistent model for performance measurement	• Enable performance measurements to be tracked in each capability area and end-to-end across the whole organization • Provide a consistent framework by which to evaluate the performance of different operational groups

When the Army general introduced above was promoted to head the entire organization, he knew firsthand that all the initiatives underway were disconnected from each other, in part because there was not a single strategy for driving success for the organization.

The general decided to cease work on all current initiatives and appointed a single person to be in charge of developing the organization's strategic metrics. He required all the subcommands to participate equally in the process under the guidance of that independent task force leader. These steps proved critical in focusing the effort, simplifying accountability, and fostering collaboration.

The result was a very clear, strategic, comprehensive, and representative set of measurable outcomes in the following areas: customer focus (readiness and quality of life), efficiency and effectiveness, sustainability, and safety.

From these outcomes, the general's team was able to derive a strategy, linked to tactics that would ultimately help him turn the organization in a direction that would allow it to succeed.

Too Much Data, Too Little Information

The goal of developing sound metrics is something that all organizations agree on, but few accomplish. In his book *The Agenda: What Every Business Must Do to Dominate the Decade*, Michael Hammer includes a chapter called "Measure Like You Mean It," which describes the importance of putting in place the right metrics to manage an organization, whether it be commercial or public sector. Hammer points out that measurements provide valuable, specific information about *current* performance in the organization, to be used to make decisions to improve the *future* performance.

Unfortunately, not many organizations "measure like they mean it." Perhaps part of the problem with effective use of data is that too much *useless* data are gathered, especially in the public sector.

Here are some sentiments we hear and lessons we can all learn:

- **"We use 2% of what we measure. The rest is CYA."** Organizations have spent extravagant amounts of time and money collecting measurements—with very little idea of what to do with any of them! A private sector telecommunications company collected 10,000 measures of a specific activity throughout the company, the great majority of which were never even looked at, much less used. Almost every organization has a similar data horror story.

  Lesson: Don't waste your organization's time and energy collecting data you won't use.

- "We measure far too much and get far too little for what we measure because we never articulated what we need to get better at, and our measures aren't tied together to support higher-level decision making." Organizations collect measurements or data without having a clear purpose and without understanding what the data actually represent or communicate.

  Lesson: First figure out what you need to know to make better operational and strategic decisions. Then determine what kind of data you'll need.

- "We are masters of the micro. We can tell you how long it takes to get a new supply of paper clips delivered but not our overall response time to customers." Many organizations have no idea what they should be measuring, so they grab on to something simple and obvious, settling for precision at a micro level rather than seeking valuable information on a broader level. They measure what is easy to measure, whether or not the measure matters.

  Lesson: Don't collect any kind of data just because it's easy to gather. Put your time and effort into getting data that will help you run your organization more effectively or efficiently.

- "If you want to know my response times on March 2nd, I'll tell you in mid-April." Many measurement systems are lagging and out of date by the time the results are presented to the managers who are supposed to make use of them.

  Lesson: Data that comes too late to help you take corrective action are useless in terms of improving performance. Work to improve your systems so you can get real-time data. If that is impossible, it's better to have a rough estimate quickly than a precise measurement when it's too late. And in some cases, you'll want to collect data that will let you predict performance, as we discussed in Chapter 4.

Do some of these complaints sound familiar? Just because the misuse of data is common doesn't mean it's acceptable. Fortunately, there are some simple steps you can take to establish a metric system that will become invaluable in helping you run your organization.

Picking the Right Performance Metrics

If the sentiments quoted above are an indication, odds are good that you can identify a lot of data that your organization is collecting just by looking around. The question you have to ask is whether any of that data is useful for the purpose of improving performance.

Remember, the goal of this book is to help you establish practices that will help you build the kind of organizational anatomy that is capable of achieving more, with lower cost and at faster speed. The purpose of metrics in this context is to give you useful information about what needs to be improved, *how* it needs to be improved, and whether the actions you're taking are having the desired impact.

Metrics are usually divided into three categories:

1. **Output metrics.** These measure something that the people who receive your group's service or product will notice: how long it takes for them to receive that output (the right answer to a question, the right form, a check, an evaluation, the right equipment, etc.), the cost to them, and/or the quality of the output (number of errors in a form, number of defects in a product). A change in an outcome metric means that something visible and important to your customers is happening.

2. **Process metrics.** These measure what is happening internally in your operations: the time needed to complete each step of a process, the number of defects per step, and so on. Ideally, the process metrics you develop will also help you improve your outcomes. For example, if you have an overall goal of lowering costs for customers, you could measure the amount of wasted materials, since those materials represent unnecessary costs that customers may be paying for.

3. **Activity metrics.** These measure the level of activity in your organization related to enabling improved performance but do not guarantee that customers will see that improvement. For example, holding public meetings may be part of your strategy for improving commu-

nication with your customers. But tracking an increase in the number of public meetings does not guarantee improved communication. You may measure how many people have completed improvement training, but simply completing the training does not mean that your organization has seen any benefit from that activity. Activity metrics may be necessary for internal management purposes but are seldom useful in improvement.

To evaluate your current level of performance, focus first on developing outcome metrics. Once you know which outcomes you want to improve, you need to identify the process metrics that are good indicators of what is happening with those outcomes.

To use metrics effectively, you need a mix of financial and non-financial performance measures that reflect a mix of service, cost, and quality levels and provide decision makers with an accurate picture of the state of operations. Performance gaps for these key indicators will lead you to focus efforts on identifying and addressing the causes. Metrics can also help you identify best practices, giving you the opportunity to replicate them across your organization.

Developing a Metric System You Will Use

Monitoring and actively managing performance using a thoughtful selection of metrics will enable you to determine whether your organization is meeting its stated financial goals and achieving the performance levels necessary for the desired strategic and mission outcomes.

The U.S. Army Medical Command (MedCom), for example, uses a Web-based Command Management System to push targets and performance goals out to commanders. This means leaders at all levels have easy access to real-time results, and the system continually reinforces the organization's main goals. The system compiles information from subordinate officers to generate a Balanced Scorecard (graphic displays of key metrics). Regular review of the scorecards has increased awareness of the gaps between actual and target performance. As one officer commented, "If the numbers show that performance hasn't shifted off the baseline for six years, you have to ask why. It's not because people weren't working hard. They were working their butts off. Seeing those same numbers quarter after quarter means we've got to reinvent ourselves."

How do you get to the point of having that kind of effective system? There is no single best way to develop and select metrics, but here are some key considerations:

- **Metrics development is an ongoing process.** There should be an expectation that metrics will change over time as business conditions and process performance change.

- **Outcome metrics should be developed from a top-down perspective.** It is the responsibility of leadership to define overall organizational success in unambiguous terms.

- **Process metrics should be developed from a bottom-up perspective.** Start with frontline staff to generate buy-in and take advantage of technical knowledge. Involve staff members in identifying metrics that they will use in the regular course of their workday. However, leadership should sit in on the development meetings to ensure that the process metrics identified link to the organization's broader business metrics and to ensure that a *system* of metrics is being developed, rather than unrelated measures.

- **Leadership should seek to promote employee involvement.** Identifying metrics in a group setting gives every idea a chance to be thoroughly discussed and vetted. Often, it will take time for a group to come together on appropriate metrics, which is OK, as long as the group is making progress toward consensus. Developing a full set of metrics may take many months.

- **Bring in the IT department early and make its staff an integral part of the team.** Decisions about what data to collect and how to organize and process them for easy review and interpretation should be made by data experts. But the systems needed to make data collection and analysis happen reliably almost always involve the IT department. The transition from design to implementation will go much more smoothly if IT representatives are involved in the discussions from the beginning. They must understand why the metrics system is a priority and how it must perform to be useful to the organization.

Developing Appropriate Metrics

To help you get started on developing your own metrics system, here is an outline of a typical metrics development and deployment process.

1. Decide what you need to measure to improve performance

Start by thinking about what you want to know, whether it is the strategic and operational impacts of projects or improvement efforts, customer responses to changes in your operations, identification of opportunities, or something else.

2. Select the metrics

In some cases, the decision about what data to collect is clearly related to what you want to know (if you want to know about late deliveries, you need to measure delivery times). In other cases, you may need to identify a

---

Tip: Making sure you get good data

Collecting data that are reliable and tells you what you want to know is part science and part art. There is a lot of information about good data collection techniques in the marketplace. Perhaps someone in your organization already knows what makes a good metric. Here is an overview of key factors to consider:

- **The data should be a reliable indicator of the outcome you're focusing on.** Make sure that the data you're collecting accurately indicates success or failure in the outcome you're interested in (customer satisfaction, cost savings, time savings, etc.).

- **The data should tell you about problems you need to solve.** If the goal is to improve performance, measuring what you do well will not move you toward that goal. You need data that reflects the problems you need to address and correct to raise your performance level.

- **Apply statistical principles** to get reliable, meaningful data. Anyone who's collected data knows that there are a lot of potential sources of error that can make data unreliable: different people can collect the data in different ways, there may be subtle sources of bias, and so on. That's why it's important to involve people who are knowledgeable about data collection practices when developing your methods.

---

number of possibilities and then narrow the list based on convenience and the strength of the relationship between the metric and your goals. For example, you may have a number of metrics potentially related to customer satisfaction, and it may take some experimentation to find the best one.

To develop both output and process metrics, you need to know something about how the processes and systems in your organization work. Determine their inputs and outputs. Look for steps or areas where knowing the cycle times would be useful or where you could collect useful data on specific issues (on errors and defects, for example). Use process maps (such as SIPOC diagrams) and root cause analysis to help you identify measurable process characteristics that are linked to what you want to know.

You can also think about what we call **UnDeR metrics**, which represent common types of problems organizations experience (see Figure 29).

Figure 29: UnDeR Metrics

UnDeR		
Un	**De**	**R**
Unavailable	Defective	Rejected
Unready	Destroyed	Reworked
Unfit	Decayed	Restricted
Unacceptable	Detained	Reviewed
Unknown	Deferred	Returned
Unanticipated		Rerouted

Once you've identified potential metrics, think about **data availability** and **feasibility**, and particularly the relationship between the two. As discussed previously, it's a mistake to focus only on data that are easy to get, because they may not be useful to you. On the flip side, you can't rely on data that are so hard to gather that collection becomes a huge hassle. We have all seen highly accurate data that are so complicated that only a few people can understand what they mean or know how to collect and analyze tgen. Make sure you get data that the people responsible for collecting and analyzing the data can and will use. Put simply, employees will either avoid or work around metrics that are difficult to collect, analyze, or understand.

Lastly, make sure you **focus on a few critical metrics.** It's easy for organizations to become overwhelmed with data. If you've identified a number of possibilities, select three to five metrics you think will be most useful.

3. Determine baselines and targets

With the metrics identified, your next step is to establish baselines and determine targets for each:

- Take a current measurement to establish a baseline.

- Establish a target value for a metric, based on the performance levels required to deliver mission value. This is the level of performance you would like to see or that you need to see for business purposes.

When possible, use **benchmarks** to develop targets. A benchmark is a high performance level that you know is achievable, used to identify, quantify, and prioritize improvement opportunities to determine which offer the greatest potential return; they also highlight areas at risk. Thus, benchmarks provide a factual basis and context for creating a business plan to drive change.

A benchmark can come from an internal source, such as the performance level achieved by another process in your organization, or from an external source, such as published world-class performance levels.

If benchmarks are not relevant or not available, establish meaningful targets on your own. What target level of performance you would need to achieve to see real progress in achieving your strategic or operational goals?

4. Implement a system for collecting, monitoring, and reacting to the metrics

All measurements must align to the organization's mission and strategic priorities. Leading practices for establishing a working system of metrics include:

1. **Prepare the workforce through education.** Communicate both the need for metrics and the ways in which they will help the organization achieve its goals and mission. Also, explain how you will help staff develop the needed skills.

149

2. Cascade the selected targets down to the work of individual business units, organization sectors, and regions (if applicable), and tie the effort to a budget allocation.

3. Align ownership, accountability, decision rights, and incentives for the metrics effort.

4. Track the data and report them regularly. The tracking and reporting of metrics should have as little impact as possible on the individuals performing the measurement processes. To make data collection painless, automate it where possible; if not, create standardized, easy-to-use templates for data that must be collected manually.

5. Take action to improve performance (closing the gap between your current performance and the target level).

6. Modify or discontinue metrics as needed. If you find that a metric does not lead to any action, it is not helping you improve. Look for an alternative.

Tip: Create a dashboard to display your key metrics

Dashboards organize and present information in a format that is easy to read and interpret. The objective of a dashboard is to provide a consolidated, transparent view across operations. To achieve this, use a standard and agreed-on set of Key Performance Indicators (KPIs). A High Performance organization leverages dashboards to allow executives and management to easily monitor KPIs for the whole organization and/or for their respective business units. KPIs should be aligned to the strategic plan, as well as the key aspects of the business process the metrics are intended to measure.

Keep Your Goal in Sight

One way to think of a metric is as a proxy for a desired outcome. You gather data for a metric in the hope of being able to better manage your organization's performance and thus serve your customers better. It is the ultimate goal—happier customers, expenses avoided, time saved—that matters, not the metric itself. Improving a desired outcome requires a metric, an accountable leader, and a focused plan that is executed by motivated and prepared employees. At the same time, the system has to be flexible enough to accommodate updates that reflect changed circumstances.

The metrics will also be the basis for project reviews (see Ch. 3). Having an infrastructure of aligned metrics means that management decisions about allocation of resources can be made with regard to how an individual project or set of projects is doing relative to a "North Star" of key issues derived from your Prime Value Chain outputs. It continually reinforces the idea that project results and metrics must be linked to the larger strategic needles.

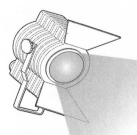

Managing Change

The most commonly cited reasons for unsuccessful organizational transformation are unexpected employee resistance to change and underestimating the difficulty of managing change. Many organizations fail to reap the expected benefits of change programs due to the lack of buy-in, commitment, and user knowledge. Yet change-support work is often under-resourced and the first to be cut when a new program or application has exceeded its budget.

Organizations often mistakenly equate change management with communications and training alone. While those elements are important, our colleagues' research shows that there are four levers in an organization that have an even bigger impact on the success of any change:

- **Leadership/sponsorship**: Whether or not there is a top-level manager or executive who takes an active role in making a project or initiative successful

- **Business processes**: The actual changes in daily work that have been made to enable improved performance

- **Collaboration**: The ease or difficulty of sharing information and working together

- **Engagement**: Degree of workforce involvement in defining and pursuing improvements

Successful leaders create a shared vision for change, gain commitment to that vision, and lead their people through all stages of transformational change. A good change model drives change both at the macro and micro levels (see Figure 30).

Figure 30: Handling Change at the Macro and Micro Levels

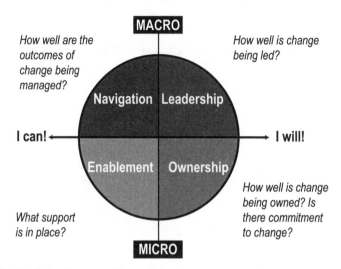

The top half of the figure addresses how to prepare the organization:

- **Navigation** includes determining the scope, sequence, and pace of the change within programs. The Navigation segment addresses how well the outcomes of the change are being managed. To ensure that the capacity for change is aligned with the pace of change, continually monitor the Navigation function.

- **Leadership** focuses on gaining commitment to and sponsorship for the program from key leaders. The Leadership segment addresses how well the change is being led. Strong leadership is required to sustain the effort or project.

The micro level of the model (lower half of Figure 30) focuses on building change readiness within an individual.

- **Enablement** focuses on building skills, knowledge, and experience so that individuals can perform their new roles more effectively. Together with the Ownership segment, Enablement helps individuals understand the support that is in place to help with the transformation.

- **Ownership** focuses on helping individuals understand the need for a change and increasing their commitment to make it happen.

Treat workforce development strategically

Another element of High Performance in government is making sure that human resource issues are evaluated in the context of your strategic priorities.

High-performing organizations create a good match between their current and future mission and their workforce. They look at the positions most critical to fulfilling their missions and make sure that the right people with the right skills are in those jobs. They have evaluated changing demands and conducted workforce and skill-building training accordingly.

Accenture research (High Performance Workforce Study, 2006) shows that the cause of workforce performance struggles can be attributed to several shortcomings in human resources management and training. These include:

- A lack of connection to business drivers
- Failure to measure the business impact of human resources and training efforts
- Ineffective or inadequate knowledge capture and sharing capabilities
- Functional leaders' inadequate involvement in people issues

Human resource and workforce development issues of those kinds are beyond the scope of this book, but we urge you to address them as you decide what it will take to create a successful workforce.

PART IV

PERFORMANCE–ORIENTED DEPLOYMENT

INTRODUCTION TO PART IV

Once again, imagine your organization 5 or 10 years out. Improvement is now an everyday occurrence. Innovations in products, services, and delivery are keeping you ahead of your customers. Staff members can easily tell whether the work they're doing is aligned to strategic priorities. Management makes decisions based on readily available metrics linked to both immediate and long-term goals. Your organization has a handle on how to anticipate changes and can respond quickly.

Now compare that future to the reality of today. There's a lot that has to happen, right? When you've created a road map of improvement projects as discussed in Part I, you have the first part—but only the first part—of the deployment picture. Chapter 9 looks at how to adapt traditional strategic planning so that it incorporates thinking that leads to a Performance anatomy—what needs to be done around Operational Excellence, agility, and culture to support business goals. Spotlight E highlights the importance of incorporating Scenario Analysis into strategic planning to help you create an agile organization. The last chapter offers some options for accelerating both deployment and the realization of results as you make the kinds of changes detailed in this book.

Special thanks to Robert McNamara, Dave Stahlman, and William Englehaupt for help in developing the content in these chapters.

CHAPTER 9

Making the Future a Reality

Augmenting strategic planning
with strategic management

A government leader told us recently, "I thought we had an understanding of our strategy. . . . But over the course of the year, we didn't really make much progress toward the objectives we put into our strategic plan." Another leader confessed that her agency's strategic plan was sitting on a shelf. "We don't really use it to guide our organization," she said.

Sound familiar? Most federal, state, and local government agencies have some version of a formal planning process built into their yearly budget cycles. The main purpose of this planning is often to justify budgets and capital requests to lawmakers and to build plans to execute the organization's mission. But even so, frustrations with strategic planning are common. Although a lot of hard work goes into the plan, it is often not used at all or is pushed aside by new priorities that arise unexpectedly, diverting the organization's attention.

Effective strategic planning is a lot more difficult than is generally acknowledged. Writing a plan that describes some goals and objectives is relatively simple, although time-consuming. What's hard is developing a plan that:

- Accurately captures where your organization is today, including its performance levels, in-house skills, capabilities, and resources

- Describes in clear terms the agreed-on future directions

- Describes how the organization will be fundamentally different in the future

- Identifies specific initiatives required to give you the capability to achieve the goals

- Defines metrics that can be used to gauge progress toward the goals

As if strategic planning isn't challenging enough, harder still is strategic *management*—practices that link everyday work to strategic goals. It is this kind of management that ensures that your organization makes progress toward the goals spelled out in your plan.

Because strategic planning and strategic management must inspire and guide change, they are essential to shaping an organization's progress along the three dimensions that are the focus of this book:

- **Operational Excellence.** The strategic plan should articulate priorities and plans so managers at all levels will know how to better allocate resources to the initiatives and activities that will provide the most value to the organization and its customers. Further, the strategic plan should describe how the organization will build the internal and customer-facing capabilities.

- **Agility.** The strategic plan and the planning process provide a grounding in the current and potential future environments within which an agency operates. An organization with its capability development aligned to future scenarios and a strong culture aligned to its mission and vision is able to *adapt* its activities. It can focus on change *before* it is forced to do so and therefore react more quickly to unanticipated events.

- **Culture.** The strategic plan clarifies the mission and describes the vision. It provides a foundation for what the organization—and the people of the organization—aspire to be. It serves as a guidepost for what is to be sought, what is valued, and what will be rewarded.

The purpose of this chapter is to present a process that will reinvigorate strategic planning in your organization, a process in which the act of creating the plan contributes as much to improved performance as the actual plan. Done correctly, strategic planning and strategic management will rally employees around a common vision and mission and help you achieve higher levels of performance.

The Good, the Bad, and the Missing

Over the past two decades, strategic planning in government has become much more sophisticated, especially at the federal level.

- U.S. government agencies are required to develop formal strategic plans through the Government Performance and Results Act of 1993 (GPRA). Under the act, organizations are charged with developing multi-year strategic plans, annual performance plans, and annual performance reports. Agencies are required to update their plans every three years.

- Many elements commonly seen in formal strategic plans of commercial organizations are now used by government agencies as part of their annual planning process. For example, the Clinger-Cohen Act shapes federal agencies' approach to IT acquisition and management. It requires that an agency have a capital budgeting and investment control process prior to making IT investments, and the agency must show a link between its strategic mission and its investment in information systems.

That's the good news.

The bad news is that strategic planning is often treated as a check-the-box activity. For too many agencies, planning has become very formal and procedural, with the goal of "completing the plan" rather than creating a plan that will actually be useful in guiding the organization's actions. In short, many government organizations have gotten good at planning but remain poor at strategizing. They put more effort into creating a long, complicated document than into the critical thinking required to develop a real plan—a recipe for creating "shelfware."

Another huge challenge is the narrow scope of vision that most government organizations adopt while planning. This is ironic, because the nature of government work often requires a broad perspective. Very few, if any, government organizations are solely responsible for addressing all aspects of a given public issue and therefore cannot achieve their mission without collaboration with or involvement by other organizations. Yet agencies too often limit their strategic planning efforts to just what happens within their

159

walls and within their budgets. This myopic approach precludes a comprehensive view of a problem and its solution and creates redundancies, conflicts, and gaps within and between other organizations.

As a result of these deficiencies in strategic planning, the missing element in the public sector is the inability to make progress on mission-critical goals. The pressures of dealing with today's burning fires distract the organization from devoting adequate time and energy to strategic issues.

To build on the good, repair or replace the bad, and fill in the missing, public sector organizations need to build a stronger system for linking daily operations to strategic priorities. That means they:

- Bring departments and employees together under a common umbrella to enable the organization to focus on its outcome goals

- Link the allocation of resources, both human and financial, to performance goals

- Support the management of the organization, monitoring performance and guiding the major investments

The characteristics of a process that can enhance the good aspects of your planning, replace the bad aspects with more effective activities, and fill in the gaps are described in the next section.

Approach Matters as Much as Output

Plans are nothing; planning is everything.
—Dwight D. Eisenhower

Plans may not be "nothing," as Eisenhower famously asserted, but we can agree that planning—the approach you take and the process you use—leads to understanding and insights that are more valuable than any specific document.

When your process is focused on producing a document, you end up with a big three-ring binder that contains a lot of details that no one will ever use. When you use an approach that's built around getting a broad, comprehensive view of your organization and is focused on generating decisions to guide the future, you will better understand the challenges you face and the changes necessary to achieve your goals. Such an approach also increases the odds that the plan will be used—whether it fills a thick binder or consists of a few PowerPoint slides. Also, greater understanding of the critical issues and decisions addressed in developing the plan will enable greater organizational flexibility—agility—when details of the plan must be changed (as they inevitably will be).

The most critical objective of any strategic planning effort in government must be that the plan is implemented. This may seem obvious, but too many plans gather dust on shelves shortly after production. Even the most brilliant vision and solutions for mission accomplishment will be ignored if there is no organizational energy or resources allocated to implementation.

A strategic plan is more likely to be used if it:

- Clearly outlines the appropriate scope and vision

- Provides a road map to develop the internal and mission capabilities needed for success

- Achieves acceptance from a broad group of internal and external stakeholders on whom success depends

- Builds in agility to enable the organization to adapt rapidly to change, based on common understandings of the organization and its objectives and organizational capabilities

The planning approach used in public sector organizations that are very effective at strategic planning and strategic management has the following characteristics:

1. Visible and active **executive-level sponsorship**

2. An intensely **collaborative** approach with stakeholders

3. An **assessment of multiple scenarios** to determine the appropriate organizational direction

4. A focus on identifying and building the organizational **capabilities** and **strengths** necessary to achieve mission success

5. **Outcome-based performance metrics** linked to the plan's goals and objectives

The processes in these organizations also include kickoff activities for the transition to implementation. But before we get to those, let's look at the planning process ingredients in more depth.

1. Executive Sponsorship

The leader who is the face of the strategic planning effort—the official **executive sponsor**—is perhaps the most critical component of the effort. That person sets the tone for the undertaking, provides access to key parties and manages their inclusion in the process, and determines the extent to which the plan will establish and articulate new aspirations for performance. The executive sponsor's attitude determines the extent to which people in the organization will be held accountable for implementation of a plan.

For those reasons, successful organizations choose a senior executive who has both credibility and authority as the sponsor of the strategic planning process. Ideally, this person will be either a member of the C-Suite or the functional or operational lead of the agency component that is carrying out the plan. The sponsor does not need to be intimately involved in every aspect of the planning process but does need to oversee the effort and provide guidance as necessary. All participants, both inside and outside the organization, need to understand that the sponsor endorses both the effort and the product.

The sponsor's role includes:

- **Communicating the goals of the process and the ultimate uses of the plan.** The sponsor's initial communications to the strategic planning team represent the foundation for the change management communications related to the plan and for any change it creates.

- **Making sure that the right people within the agency are involved in the effort.** The executive sponsor needs to bring together the right team—with the right mandate—to make the planning effort a success. The planning will be more effective when undertaken in close collaboration with executives and frontline personnel (including both field and headquarters staff), and when it represents a balanced mix of perspectives. Many organizations create dedicated strategic planning leadership teams to bring diverse personnel together to conduct or oversee the strategic planning effort.

- **Defining the scope of the strategic planning effort**, especially as it may extend beyond the organization's boundaries. Is the strategic planning effort for only a specific office or agency, or will the plan create a vision and road map for a group of organizations (an enterprise) that should—no, *must*—work together to achieve the desired end state? The sponsor stakes his or her political and personal capital on the effort of forging new relationships and spearheading collaboration with other public and private sector organizations, especially if the vision faces significant bureaucratic barriers.

- **Setting the tone for effective implementation.** It is the sponsor's clarity of vision and belief that the planning effort will shape future agency performance that will keep the work from becoming simply an intellectual exercise. As upcoming sections will demonstrate, implementation efforts must be driven by solid outcome-based performance measures that are linked to individual performance plans.

- **Leading by example.** Visually demonstrating, embracing, and practicing the concepts and components of change. The leader makes it clear to all that she or he sees the initiative as the way works get done at all levels, especially at the sponsor's level.

What it takes to be transformational

The challenges facing many government organizations are so great that in many cases a strategic plan has to define a transformation, not just a change. Common strategic planning efforts focus internally, but successful, transformational strategic plans position the agency within the broader enterprise of organizations that work together to achieve common goals. The sponsor must establish and communicate this vision of enterprise-wide collaboration from the outset, defining the vision and the outcomes (where appropriate) that will be the measures of success for the entire enterprise.

---

2. Stakeholder Collaboration

Effective strategic planning is a mix of top-down and bottom-up ideas and input. Top-down approaches provide structure and clarity around a mission and objectives and identify and enforce new ways of doing and thinking about work. Bottom-up ideas ground the effort in the career experiences of employees. Engaging many types of people in the planning process provides valuable insight and helps staff members feel that they are part of the process and part of the solution. Such involvement greatly facilitates the organizational changes to come.

As mentioned in a previous chapter, one of the greatest drawbacks of strategic planning in public sector organizations is the tendency to plan and execute within stovepipes. The most obvious stovepipes are organizational, with people working only with others in their organization. The pitfalls of this approach are well documented, especially as related to security operations. But stovepipes can also be psychological, with agency employees constantly reverting to the customary way of approaching and solving problems, believing that if it's not invented here, it won't work.

Changing the process of strategic planning to get a better strategic plan therefore has to include clear and meaningful steps to break down stovepipes and to encourage communication among three key groups:

- **Customers**. This group includes both the end users and the implementers of the plan; that is, both constituents and employees. You need to engage customers early in formulating strategy (and subsequently in developing solutions) to sharpen the focus of your activities and help you deliver a product or service that provides better access and greater benefit to them.

- **Partners**. These are the peer groups, offices, or organizations with related missions whose cooperation you need to ensure delivery on your mission. High Performance organizations take a broad, holistic view of business challenges and engage fellow agencies to collaborate across common or complementary business processes. You will need to identify these stakeholders early in your planning process and invite them to the table for the strategic planning effort. That will help you:
  - Identify complementary capabilities and processes
  - Create simple and logical ways to divide the work that will be obvious to your constituents or customers
  - Improve efficiencies by eliminating redundancies and applying complementary capabilities

Conversely, failing to engage these partners during planning creates redundant, stovepiped solutions that are expensive to integrate and confusing for customers to navigate.

Partner collaboration

An example of successful collaboration across government entities is the U.K. prime minister's Strategy Unit. Data collection, forecasting, and planning are done across the whole of government. Since the Strategy Unit is an independent organization, strategic planning continues across government administrations, thus allowing the implementation of plans spanning long time frames.

- **Contributors.** These are organizations from both the public and private sector that have the knowledge, skills, or capability you need to better deliver on your mission. Connecting to contributors can help you learn about global best practices that will help solve your challenges. It may be common wisdom to think of these connections as simply engaging private sector vendors, but the options are broader than that.

  Focusing on capabilities available through contributor organizations will help you better assess and meet your needs and give you the opportunity to see solutions in action. For example, if a core capability needed by your organization is financial claims processing, it can be very valuable to speak first to financial firms whose regular business depends on similar processing. Along with discussions with vendors who may integrate such solutions, this analysis can help agencies understand the outcomes and the organizational impacts these solutions might produce. Engaging at least some best-practice providers early in the planning process is critical for developing solutions that are not only best-in-government but on a par with the best in the world.

One example of this type of engagement and communication is the US-VISIT program, which supports the Department of Homeland Security. US-VISIT has been a leader in deploying advanced biometric capabilities in very challenging environments with stringent operational requirements.

The organization has become successful by working closely with the technical community as potential contributors, drawing on organizations and people who can work together to understand the art of the possible, and using these associations to push vendors to develop innovative solutions where "the possible" didn't quite meet the business need.

3. Scenario Analysis

Planning for a single hoped-for or "official" future rarely is successful.

Except by strange coincidence or extremely rare good fortune, the future will never hold exactly what agency leadership expects. The typical dilemma that planners face is that all their knowledge is about the past, but all their decisions are about the future. Pulitzer Prize recipient George Will captured this dilemma when he wrote, "The future has a way of arriving unannounced."

Many traditional strategic planning efforts address just one officially sanctioned future, which is usually a time-limited straight-line projection of current trends carried into the future. The official future is often built through simple forecasts or budget or accounting projections. These straight-line projections are often useless because planners do not have an effective understanding of the variables at play and the relationships among them. Also, few planners look at whether the variables that influence an organization and its operating environment today will continue to be important in the future.

Straight-line planning can work in the short term but does not have the flexibility to respond to change. A single, static, official future has a very short shelf life.

An organization needs to be able to adapt effectively to changes in its operating environment, new customer demands, and expansion in its mission without degrading its performance. To accomplish this, you need to incorporate **Scenario Analysis** into your strategic planning. Scenario Analysis is a structured process in which you explore multiple futures and determine which capabilities and priorities are most relevant to those futures. You also test how a proposed strategy holds up in various future states. (For more on how to perform Scenario Analysis in a way that will enhance your strategic planning efforts, see Spotlight D.)

4. Focus on Capabilities

Too often, strategic plans focus on only one issue: *what*.

That narrow focus is one reason why so many plans sit on the shelf. After identifying an impressive vision and specific goals, no action is taken because there is no common understanding of *how* to achieve the lofty goals. The challenge can leave organizations uncertain about where to start. Also, it's likely some goals will appear to be mutually exclusive. For example, the goal "facilitate border crossings" would likely conflict with "improve border security." Similarly, "improve revenue collection" might seem to take an opposite direction from "improve customer satisfaction." If the organization can't find solutions that will accomplish multiple goals simultaneously, it's unlikely that progress will be made on any of them.

That's why effective strategic planning answers not just *what* but also *how* and *when*. The added questions force you to identify specific areas in which your organization must excel in order to achieve your vision.

For example, one agency's facilities management office created a strategic plan to improve its ability to support frontline personnel. The plan meant that the organization would need to fundamentally re-evaluate its core mission and goals and the organizational capabilities needed to achieve them. The plan included an assessment of technology, business processes, and human capital needs and solutions, resulting in a road map of how and when objectives would be achieved. One component, project management, was identified as a necessary capability. It then became much easier to focus on identifying technology tools, business process improvements, and the training and cultural enhancements necessary to enhance that capability. This approach contrasts with less-structured planning activities that result in a laundry list of improvement strategies rather than a plan.

The capabilities you identify will likely be a mix of core mission areas (e.g., intelligence analysis, biometric identification, claims processing)and critical internal support areas (e.g., data management, project management). A **capability framework** that identifies capabilities needed to deliver on your mission enables you to:

- Change your mind-set on how to deliver service ("We need to be less like a government bureaucracy and more like a bank.")

167

- Allow you to identify best practices to emulate ("How does the credit card industry identify and combat fraud?")

- Apply and coordinate complementary stakeholder capabilities ("Agency X is already able to determine customer and constituent identity and eligibility, so why should we re-create that capability? Let's just partner with that agency.")

- Create the framework for the portfolio of implementation activities ("To achieve our objectives, we need to enhance our capabilities in x, y, and z.")

- Identify and plan specific improvement actions that build capabilities through enhancements to business process design, technology tools, or the skills and behaviors of the workforce.

Using a capability framework as a base, tangible, specific projects can be identified, evaluated, and initiated, and improvement actions can be clearly focused, coordinated, and linked to the overall improvement plan.

5. Outcome-Based Performance Metrics

Chapter 8 pointed out that *what gets measured gets done*. Identifying performance metrics has to become a standard element in strategic planning.

During the development of the plan itself, it is unlikely that the full performance management structure (with all its accompanying metrics and targets) will be determined. However, the planning phase is the ideal time to establish the foundation of the measurement and management framework.

This foundation should be based on three key considerations:

- The goals and objectives should be customer-centric (that is, define what improvements are needed to provide better products or services to your customers). Success should depend on improving the experience of people who use your service or product.

- While goals may be aspirational—represent a level of achievement far beyond your current performance—you need to define specific objectives.

- Every objective should be accompanied by outcome metrics. You'll need to cascade the objectives and metrics throughout the organization's hierarchy.

Organizations commonly struggle with the challenge of applying metrics to their highest goals, because societal outcomes are very challenging to measure directly. But if you don't have metrics related to those goals, you will have a gap in your measurement framework. To address this challenge, it is often best to look for subordinate, more readily measured objectives related to the aspirational goal. For example, an agency with an aspirational goal of reducing high school dropout rates might focus on an outcome metric of improved reading scores in middle school. An agency charged with improving the health of newborns could look at participation in prenatal care programs. Specific numerical targets can be set as part of annual performance plans but need not be explicitly stated in the overall plan, though many organizations do include their numerical targets.

When this top-level framework is complete, it is necessary to add metrics to track the accomplishment of lower-order activities, their results, and the progress toward goals. A full hierarchy of cascading metrics is usually developed only after the initial strategic planning phase, but it is often valuable to consider them when developing the strategies to be included in the plan. What are the measurable subordinate activities and results that make accomplishment of the objectives possible? How can these cause-and-effect relationships be analyzed and planned to create actionable strategies? And, once implementation begins, how can measurement of results provide insight into underlying successes and challenges?

What is an outcome-based metric?

Throughout this book, we have used the term "outcome" to mean the end result of a process or series of processes. In government, that would be the benefits or consequences for your customers, stakeholders, or the public at large. An outcome-based metric does not measure what your organization does (its activities); it instead assesses the *impact* of those activities, such as improved safety, health, education, economic stability, or whatever is appropriate according to your mission.

Performance-Oriented Strategic Planning

While the strategic planning approach outlined above can serve as a guide, you may not have the capacity or resources to conduct all the analyses or activities referenced, nor should you always do so. Rather, pick the analyses most relevant to your organization and delegate the investigation and number crunching to others.

The ultimate goal is to move from *static strategic planning*, where a plan is done once and then remains unchanged for a year or two (likely becoming obsolete the day it is released), to *dynamic strategic planning,* where regular reviews ensure that the plan is kept updated and therefore meaningful in terms of reaching the organization's goals.

Although every organization is unique, several lessons learned from high-performing government organizations can be incorporated into your strategic planning approach and process:

- **Participation.** Have executive sponsors lead and participate in the strategic planning process; include executives from across the organization, especially those who will be responsible for implementing specific initiatives

- **Multiple sources of information.** Use multiple sources of external information and analysis to challenge conventional thinking, generate robust operating scenarios for analysis, and help drive better executive decisions

- **Value and expectations.** Focus on value, as defined by mutual or common stakeholder perspectives, and assess whether the strategy will enable the organization to achieve the performance expectations for these stakeholders

- **Capabilities review and assessment.** Integrate review and assessment of capabilities into the strategic planning process to help you identify where you need partners and contributors and what internal capabilities you need to develop further to execute the plan successfully

- **Initiatives.** Launch the initiative during the strategic planning process to gain traction; align the initiative clearly to the strategic goals and performance metrics

- **Execution requirements.** Keep execution requirements in mind so the strategy will be practical and executable in light of the organization's culture and capabilities

Using a Strategic Plan to Manage Your Organization

One agency we have worked with is working hard to improve its strategic planning at multiple levels. Many of its offices have followed the guidelines above to develop more robust plans. Nonetheless, implementation is a challenge for some offices within this agency, with unexpected priorities and pressures stealing attention from what were identified in the plans as priorities. But other offices have been able to use the plans to manage their organization.

One of the major offices, for example, is using its plan as a guidebook for improvement across six capability areas. Goals and capabilities spelled out in the plan are used as the basis for everything from hiring to measuring.

Pitfalls in strategic planning

As with many management approaches, strategic planning and formulation present pitfalls that should be avoided:

- Not using the planning process to align the strategy to organization beliefs and values
- Failure to identify and focus on important strategic issues
- Inefficient stakeholder and constituent analysis
- Failure to involve business units in the planning process
- Lack of methods for monitoring progress against the strategic plan
- Basing decisions primarily on the potential benefits of initiatives without sufficient recognition of the risks
- Too much attention to tactical issues; insufficient attention to strategic issues
- Under-appreciation of execution requirements and inadequate assessment of company capabilities

A governance board of senior executives meets monthly to discuss cross-organizational initiatives that were built into the strategy, evaluate performance, and identify key issues that must be resolved to meet targets. This creates a very dynamic management process that continually examines the strategy and the status of key initiatives and looks at where adjustments may be needed.

This agency's approach illustrates how management practices *after the plan is complete* need to change to make sure the organization is making progress toward it goals. To make that happen, leaders have to think about implementation from day one:

- **Involving stakeholders and employees in the planning prompts buy-in during implementation.** Successful improvement efforts are done *with* employees and constituents, rather than *to* them. This collaboration gives the various stakeholders a sense of ownership of the process and results, even if they don't agree completely with every provision. Areas of potential resistance can be identified during the planning process and plans for countermeasures put in place well before they are needed. The collaborative discussions with stakeholders then become the foundation of both the broader communications roll-out and the organizational change management efforts undertaken after formal implementation begins.

- **Linking individual performance metrics and plans to implementation targets.** Core stakeholders, especially internal agency executives, must understand that the transformation effort embodied in the plan is real. This is best made clear through alignment of individual performance plans to the performance-measurement framework developed in the planning process. Linking individual performance to specific mission outcomes, implementation milestones, or organizational improvement metrics aligns incentives and creates a strong stake in the outcome. The executive sponsor plays a critical role in championing this alignment, assigning the metrics, and rallying the organization to these shared incentives.

- **Including a clear road map with implementation targets and mission outcomes.** Every plan needs an implementation timeline, at least at a high level. Some agencies prefer that the official plan show less detail than was actually created during the planning process so that they can retain flexibility and better manage implementation communications. Further, it isn't likely that full details of the implementation will be developed as early as the initial strategic planning process.

For example, much strategic planning success was accomplished at the U.S. Department of Agriculture, where even today the organization is implementing and executing a plan that was developed years ago. Following the plan has given the agency better results, because throughout execution the overarching plan has been tied to outcomes at lower levels.

Making Progress Where It Matters

After conducting a strategic planning process based on the principles outlined in this book, an agency leader commented, "You taught me how to think about my organization. . . . Because of going through a more rigorous process, we had a much better understanding of who we were, and what we needed to do to achieve our goals."

Ironically, we often hear another, quite different reaction: "This plan doesn't tell us anything we didn't already know." While that may be true in some ways, even if the plan captures what you believe to be common knowledge, the fact is that what's in the plan *wasn't* common knowledge until it was put into writing.

Doing strategic planning right takes just as much skill as any other advanced practice your organization uses. The principles we've outlined are much more comprehensive, both in the process and the outputs, than the planning that takes place in most organizations. At the end of this process, you don't end up with just a nice presentation or a nicely organized binder but with a document that is going to capture the reasons that your business operates as it does today and the levers you need to pull to create better, more, or different results.

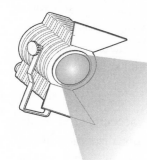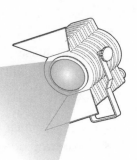

Scenario Analysis

Anticipating multiple futures

*Change is the law of life. And those who look only to the past
or present are certain to miss the future.*

—*John F. Kennedy*

No one can anticipate the future with 100% certainty. But with the right tools, you can create scenarios that capture several *likely* futures.

Private sector organizations may be inclined to bet a portion of their capital on one or more likely future markets to capitalize on market opportunities. They consider such investments as part of a broader portfolio strategy.

Public sector entities, however, have a different risk profile and limited authority and capital to invest in different potential futures, especially any that fall far outside the scope of their core mission responsibilities. Instead, they need to make selective investments in potential futures that are related to their core activities. Public sector leaders may consider these more "hedges" than "bets." Regardless, these investments in uncertain futures represent tradeoffs and prioritization choices that translate into actions they can take today that will better position their organizations for tomorrow.

A public sector organization that wants to be robust and agile has to strive for a combination of short-term responsiveness to day-to-day needs, medium-term adaptation to emerging opportunities and challenges, and long-term influence over the shape of future operating environments.[10] To achieve that goal, an organization cannot focus on just one potential future.

For example, the *forwardDallas!* Comprehensive Plan uses a community's vision and priorities to develop guidelines for Dallas's future development and strategies to help achieve those goals. The plan focuses on guiding and integrating three elements:

- *Land use.* Working strategically to stabilize existing residential neighborhoods and to accommodate growth, housing needs, and development patterns

- *Transportation.* Using roads efficiently, reducing congestion, and supporting development around public transit stations

- *Economic development.* Supporting business recruitment and retention, retail growth, and small business development

To develop this plan, the city of Dallas held public workshops where residents shared their ideas about how Dallas should grow. The team also gathered a wide range of data on past trends in demographics, economy, land use, and so on, which were used to help project how the city would change by 2030. Based on the workshop results and data, model plans called "growth scenarios" were developed, providing an overview of how future growth might affect different areas of the city. Examining the scenarios and comparing their consequences to goals and values identified through citizen input helped the planning group make recommendations that would best position Dallas for the future.

As with the Dallas effort, strategic planning in agile organizations looks out over a long time frame and examines different possibilities for the future. That effort improves the organization's ability to adapt to emerging changes and allows senior leaders to think about whether changes need to be made in anything from specific products or services offered to staffing levels in different areas to the basic operating model the organization uses.

Agile agencies rely more on *anticipatory learning* than *shock learning* to drive planning: they are proactive in looking into the future to anticipate changes and potential reactions rather than waiting until a major shock comes along and trying to react in the moment.

While there may be just one official future defined in a vision or strategic plan, agile organizations hedge their bets by developing alternative scenarios. In fact, some organizations actually monitor a number of options, developing a "strategic portfolio" to allow them to try out

If your agency or department relies on a static, one-future strategic plan, it's time to develop strategic options through Scenario Analysis. The analysis can help you develop additional insight into factors that may affect your future—and therefore your current plans, especially in relation to factors that may be just over your current planning horizon.

The long history of Scenario Analysis

Scenario Analysis is not just the latest consulting fad. Developed at the Rand Corporation for the military after World War II, it was adapted by futurist Herman Kahn in the 1960s as a business tool. Its most prominent use was by Pierre Wack and Ted Newland at Royal Dutch/Shell in the 1970s in their examination of the impact of potential scenarios on oil prices. The company is currently looking at scenarios for the year 2050 to guide long-range planning and help it shape the debate over energy policy. Since the late 1990s, Shell has created two to three scenarios a year as part of that process.

Scenario Analysis in a Nutshell

The basic premise of Scenario Analysis is that it is better to get the future **imprecisely right** than **precisely wrong**. We know that our predictions of the future are never exact. Rather than picking one definitive future and planning for that future, scenario analysis considers multiple possibilities. The organization can then test approaches and policies to see how they work under multiple likely futures and identify those that are most adaptable to different circumstances.

Scenarios do not describe a single forecasted end state. Scenarios are:

- Stories with events, actors, and motivations that describe future conditions and convey a range of possible outcomes. They lay out the contours of a possible future, like topography maps of a new territory.

- Neutral, in that they do not prescribe a particular course of action for an organization to follow.

Good scenarios become a tool that an organization can use to test its approach and make modifications long before the possible future is realized. The scenarios enable the organization to focus more on anticipating and preparing for change than on reactive responses to the unexpected.

Most scenario analysis is relatively low tech. Although computer simulations are useful, scenario analysis incorporates a *qualitative view*—participants' judgments are based not on just data modeling but also on analytical thinking rooted in whatever facts are clear and on informed intuition. Scenario builders say that the future can be known with the right blend of deep perception and intellectual rigor and that the analysis effort requires critical, creative, convergent, and divergent thinking on the issue.

Four Steps of Scenario Analysis

Scenario Analysis has four steps:

1. Describe potential future states

2. Create alternative scenarios

3. Assess performance requirements for each scenario

4. Translate the assessment into actions

Step 1. Describe Potential Future States

Although the future can't be predicted with 100% accuracy, it is possible to generate alternative perspectives on various factors that will drive the future. These factors can then be correlated to a broad range of possibilities. Important factors for consideration in the public sector will likely include some of the following, plus other factors unique to your organization's mission:

- Economy (macro, micro, and fiscal impacts)

- Demographics

- Public health

- Policy, including changes in elected administrations

- Global relationships

- Environment and climate

- Technology

Each of the factors has ranges of variability and a dependency on time. For example, demographics are fairly predictable, but determining which technology trend will dominate in 5 to 10 years is less certain. In addition, the further out you try to project, the greater the variation will be in the future states. Organizations have to determine which factors are most relevant for their industry and how to incorporate them into scenarios.

Step 2. Create Alternative Scenarios

After developing perspectives on possible future states, planners can combine the elements into scenarios. For example, one scenario may combine future states of strong economy, improved public health, and rapid technology innovation, along with other factors. Another scenario could represent a long-term future state that is radically different from the present; for example, a future without conventional warfare for the Army or one without physical mail for the U.S. Postal Service.

During the Scenario Analysis, planners can construct several scenarios that combine factors for future assessment. For each of the scenarios, probabilities can then be assigned based on the analysis and the perspective of leadership. In addition, it is important for external stakeholders involved in the strategic planning process to use the scenario development process to challenge management's thinking and bring their perspectives into the process.

Step 3. Assess Performance Requirements in Each Scenario

The strategic planning team can model the organization's performance in each scenario, based on the initial strategic goals and initiatives. Of course, the right measures need to be in place to evaluate scenario effectiveness. In addition, each scenario may require additional capabilities that the organization may not have. If your organization is unable to accomplish its mission independently in one or more scenarios, you may need to modify or create new partner relationships. Executives will find that the overall performance and effectiveness of the organization varies with the scenario and that more resources (a constant constraint) may be required to maintain or improve performance.

Step 4. Translate the Assessment into Actions

The action sets required in one scenario might be completely different from the action sets that come out of another. Differences are more likely as the time horizon expands. As the planning team reviews scenarios, team members should identify and capture the commonalities across scenarios and create strategies to build capabilities that address them. When multiple scenarios are under review, leadership will need to weigh the probability that each will exist and make tradeoffs about which actions to consider and which will generate a higher likelihood of moving the organization in the optimal direction. Once a list of actions has been defined, prioritized, and rationalized—it can be exhaustive and will require significant decision making—the team can focus on the capabilities required to support execution of those actions.

Scenario Analysis versus what-if planning

Scenario Analysis is generally considered more robust than what-if planning or other approaches that address only single elements or contingencies. Scenario Analysis is similar to the scientific approach employed in continuous improvement methods, except that only strategies that survive scenario testing can be trusted as robust and responsive.

The Case for Scenario Analysis

Scenario Analysis brings three desirable attributes to planning inside a governmental organization[11]:

- **Long view.** Governments are in business for the long term, but their planning tools tend to work best in the short range. An agency's agenda is typically driven by the emerging needs of its constituents and stakeholders. Scenario thinking, however, requires looking beyond immediate demands and peering far enough into the future to seek out new possibilities, opportunities, and challenges, many of which cannot be seen easily from today's perspective.

- **Outside-in thinking.** Most agencies do not spend a lot of time thinking about things they cannot control. Their focus is on those things they can affect inside their own organizations and with their immediate constituents. This inside-out view of the world can blindside organizations to change. Scenario Analysis forces organizations to look at the broad picture, to "bring the outside in" as they develop descriptions of potential futures. Outside-in thinking can inspire imaginative thoughts about a range of potential changes and strategies that may not have been visible otherwise.

- **Multiple perspectives.** Because there is no single "right" scenario, the process allows differing points of view to be incorporated in the planning process, reflecting the reality that governments always have to deal with multiple groups of stakeholders. The scenario process creates a powerful platform for multiple (and often divergent) perspectives, values, and opinions to come together. The result is an expansion of an organization's peripheral vision and an awareness of threats and opportunities that otherwise may have been missed. Thus,

---

Do you need Scenario Analysis?

We strongly urge all government agencies to include Scenario Analysis in their strategic planning process. That said, Scenario Analysis is particularly useful...

- In situations where there is a desire to deal with challenges proactively, for example, when there are leadership changes and major decisions impending

- In situations where changes in the organization's operating environment are recognized but not well understood; this is often the case in the face of major economic, political, and social changes or new emerging technologies

Understanding these factors, and the amount of influence they may have will help an agency deal more effectively with unlikely or unpredictable events the changes may bring.

---

scenario-building and analysis can reduce the defensiveness that sometimes arises in conventional strategic planning; it allows people to think about the future in a more inclusive forum with less blinkered and prejudiced eyes.

Scenario Analysis also allows an organization to test its strategy against the challenge of responding to external factors, be they economic, social, political, technological, or environmental. Scenarios also provide the organization with a common language, shared assumptions, and reference points for talking about the future and the longer-term challenges it faces.

The purpose of Scenario Analysis is not to pinpoint future events but to highlight large-scale forces that can push your organization's future in different directions. It's about making these forces visible, so that if they do gain strength, you will be able to recognize what's happening more quickly and make better decisions today. While it has been said that, "Those who do not learn from the past are doomed to repeat it," it may be more truthful to say that, "Those who do not learn from the future are doomed—period."

CHAPTER 10

Next-Generation Deployment Strategies

Alternate paths to speed, customization, and a solid ROI

Given all the challenges facing the public sector, three themes have emerged as critical for deploying successful efforts to build a Performance anatomy:

- **Return on investment.** Making sure that projects generate the greatest possible performance improvement in your ability to deliver your mission in less time, at lower cost, and with fewer resources and to deliver additional products and services without sacrificing quality or customer satisfaction. Reaching for this goal also ensures that your efforts will pay for themselves several times over, not only returning the initial investment but freeing up funds for further projects, service enhancements, and the like.

- **Customization to culture and environment.** There is no one-size-fits-all recipe for deployment success. What worked in another organization may not work in yours, and vice versa. That's why it helps to have the ability to adapt a deployment to better fit the culture and norms of your organization, specifically with regard to your starting point (level of maturity around improvement and change, specific challenges you face, urgency for results, conflicting initiatives, and so on).

- **Speed to execution.** All improvement efforts start out as a bunch of good ideas. Ultimately, you will make selections and changes to generate a benefit for your organization. In past years, the lag between improvement ideas and results could be months, even years. Today, an organization has to get results much faster, within a few weeks at most. Seeing a quick return on your investment—whether in the form of improved service, reduced cost, faster turnaround, and so on—can help convince your organization that the new approaches you're trying to adopt have real value. That cultural alignment will prove invaluable as you move forward.

These three themes provide the basis for evaluating the pathways for building a Performance anatomy. Many options have evolved from strategies that have been used for more than a quarter century to deploy performance improvement programs. The basic problem has always been the same: how to get from where you are now to a future state of higher performance. You will need to develop the capability to embed new skills and thought patterns into the organization, if you want to see the kind of impact that comes when every effort contributes in some degree to resolving a problem or advancing an improvement that is a priority to your organization.

The question then becomes what kind of route will provide an optimal pathway to the desired endpoint (see Figure 31). Every organization will have to find a path that provides the right mix of attacking issues (to achieve a short-term gain) and building internal capability for higher performance (to achieve long-term gains).

Figure 31: Deployment Approach Options

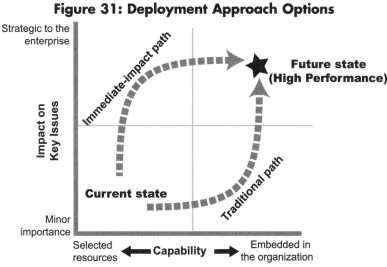

The **traditional path** labeled at the right side of the figure can be represented by the majority of Lean Six Sigma deployments conducted over the past two decades. The path moves horizontally at first—building capability—based on the widely held belief that broad, sustainable change can be achieved only when a critical mass of employees has acquired sufficient improvement skills. The traditional path typically begins with funneling large numbers of employees through multi-week classroom training. Students work on training projects chosen by themselves or their managers, usually with the purpose of solving some issue of importance to their work area—but without regard for any possible link to strategic priorities. An impact on strategic issues (the section where the line curves upward) comes "eventually," once improvement methods have taken hold.

At the opposite extreme is the **immediate-impact pathway** (upper arrow). Here, projects are executed based on their immediate impact, with little consideration given to building the internal capability for improvement. This type of effort usually involves outsourcing project leadership to third parties. The initial MRAP deployment introduced in Chapter 1 followed this path; addressing the immediate issue was so important that building capability had to take a back seat. Many other public sector organizations have taken this path, readily admitting (publicly or tacitly) that they have no intention of building internal capability.

This chapter describes three paths that represent the next-generation take on how to move from the current state to a future High Performance state (see Figure 32, next page). The first two paths are based on the traditional and immediate-impact pathways described above but with modifications that make them more effective. A third path cuts a diagonal path on the chart, reflecting the attempt to maintain a fluctuating balance between immediate impact and building internal capability. We call these paths:

1. **Assessment-Enhanced Traditional Approach.** An essentially traditional approach that focuses on building capability, with extra effort up front to assess exactly which capabilities need strengthening to best support your organization's mission

2. **Issue-Based Deployment Approach.** Similar to the upper path in Figure 31, except there is a more sophisticated approach linking projects to an issue of strategic importance

3. **Rapid Path to Results.** A path that balances rapid impact with capability-building by executing strategically linked projects through a series of Kaizens (rapid improvement events)

Figure 32: Three New Paths

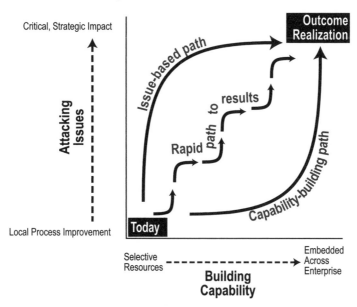

Each of these pathways has its own purpose and merits, as described below. We will also review a specific example of issue-based deployment (Path 2) that is related to getting higher value from technology.

Path 1: Assessment-Enhanced Traditional Path

When a government organization that provides immigration services decided to push for much higher levels of performance, it conducted a maturity assessment in which it compared the current state of its improvement practices to ideas from organizations that had already achieved significant success. Following the assessment, the leadership team built the organization's transformation program around the exposed gaps. Because this organization knew what "ideal" performance looked like, leaders had a much better idea of what they needed to strive for and were able to move from the assessment phase of deployment to execution much more quickly than usual.

The initial assessment in the Verification Division, for example, was based around six organizational components:

- Strategy and leadership
- Value stream management
- Talent and knowledge management
- Communication
- Organization structure and governance
- Culture

Each component was accompanied by the descriptions of different levels of performance. To get the highest rating across all the components, the Verification Division would have to:

- **Clearly articulate a compelling mission** that centered on value created for the public and outlined strategic goals for achieving that mission

- **Focus on the needs of clients and customers**, identifying their requirements and involving them in setting priorities and improved service design, measuring performance, and reporting on progress to promote transparency and accountability

- **Clarify links between inputs, processes, outputs, and outcomes**, defined so that each can be planned and designed effectively

- **Integrate a performance management system** into everyday work practices, allowing measurements of performance, cost-effectiveness, and other outcomes and fostering a culture of performance and achievement

- **Develop strategic partnerships** with stakeholders and other government agencies so it could achieve complex outcomes or outcomes outside the agency's direct control

- **Reshape its workforce and culture** in a determined effort to identify the skills and competencies needed by the organization; have a plan for effective recruiting, training and development, and retention; ensure strong, sustained, visionary leadership

Information gathered from the assessment was then used to develop targets and plans for developing capabilities linked to strategic priorities.

Path 2A: Issue-Based Deployment

A traditional capability-building path toward higher performance can be characterized early on as "a mile wide and an inch deep." The focus is on developing widespread capability by giving a lot of people experience in leading projects and solving problems. The efforts are widely dispersed.

A trend we see as organizations push to improve return on investment (ROI), customization, and speed is to reverse that formula to an "inch wide and a mile deep"—that is, to devote all their attention to a single strategic problem.

Such issued-based deployments usually start with a short strategic assessment to select the right issue or process to go "mile deep" on. Even if the leaders think they know what strategic problem to work on, the assessment generates data they can use to identify just how broad and deep the organization needs to go and to flesh out the optimal path forward. Bypassing the strategic assessment and going with gut feeling tends to leave the organization second-guessing: have we focused on the right issue?

Path 2B: Technology Value Realization

When compliance and cost efficiency were the main drivers for technology system implementation, any added business value was an afterthought. Yet technology systems represent some of the most significant capital investments that an organization will make, even without factoring in the continued focus and energy from stakeholders.

Today, although compliance is still a major driver, the value of using enterprise systems to enable and support business processes has been recognized by IT and business users alike. But research through the Accenture Institute for High Performance Business has shown that less than 5% of organizations achieve the full benefit of IT projects and investments. Fewer than half of all organizations claim to have achieved a majority of the business potentials of their IT implementations.

Achieving the value described in a business case is not guaranteed through implementation of systems alone or even with the addition of good project management. If your organization faces implementation of a large technology program, you can improve your odds of realizing greater potential value if you treat the technology initiative as a special case of an issue-based deployment. The issue in this case is the technology implementation. Four activities can be integrated into a systems implementation to help you realize the full benefit of your technology investments and become a High Performance organization.

1. **Value realization strategy.** It is important to establish early on the drivers of business performance and how those drivers are enabled by process and technology. This information is needed to guide the approach to process and technology development. A majority of processes in any organization are **non-core**: important to the organization's operations but not a source of competitive advantage or differentiation. The non-core processes lend themselves to standardization based on leading practices. In contrast, it is typically a subset of these processes that have the potential to create standout performance and advantage. Based on their potential impact, these processes are candidates for optimization or innovation. Part of the strategy must be to establish formal governance and accountability for tracking decisions and results to ensure that innovations deliver on the benefits and results that were initially targeted.

2. **Process optimization/simplification.** Organizations often make the mistake of using technology to automate ineffective business processes. This approach not only masks the causes of poor process performance but can cause poor practices to become more firmly entrenched. In our experience, a good technology solution becomes even better when process improvement techniques are used selectively to:

   - Eliminate unnecessary complexity, for which the business and customers are not willing to pay
   - Look across functional boundaries for hidden sources of waste that hinder value streams
   - Leverage information sooner to eliminate low-value downstream activities and enhance process quality

3. **Value acceleration.** Investments in technology often represent size-able cash outlays. Typical business-case scenarios assume that benefits accrue only *after* the technology goes live, which may mean payback isn't seen for many months or even a year or more. Our experience is that approximately 30% or more of business benefits can be achieved through process improvement done prior to investing in and implementing technology. Thus, a technology investment represents an attractive opportunity to accelerate benefits and improve the cash-flow profile for the investment. Additionally, the early process improvements enable organizations to reduce the risk of testing and to acclimate themselves to internal change processes.

4. **Lean technology.** The use of a proven Operational Excellence methodology such as Lean is a requirement for a successful technology development and implementation program. Even with a well-defined process, however, there are often very real opportunities along the way to improve execution and performance of these complex programs. Proven process-optimization approaches, like Lean Six Sigma, can be applied to program processes to reduce delivery cost and time, improve quality, and reduce risk. This approach has yielded benefits in areas such as increased design throughput, reduced man-days per functional process design, reduced time to complete acceptance testing, and reduced schedule time for deliverables sign-off.

Path 3: Rapid Path to Results

If neither of the previous paths appeals to your leadership team, a third alternative is an approach designed to generate results quickly while also building capability a little at a time. This path tackles a *sequence* of strategically chosen issues, creating the zigzag or step-like pattern shown in Figure 32. We call this alternative the Rapid Path to Results because it generates measurable impact more quickly than a purely traditional path and leads to capability development faster than a purely issue-based path.

The path begins with conducting a rapid, focused assessment to create a customized road map that meets the specific needs and culture of the organization. Each step of the zigzag encompasses one five-day workshop (of flexible size and focus) in which participants create a value stream map and receive just-in-time instruction on the specific methods and tools that will help them tackle a narrowly defined issue. In this way, every workshop combines project execution, issue analysis, and training. The structure of the workshops is shown in Figure 33.

Figure 33: Structure of the Rapid Path Workshop

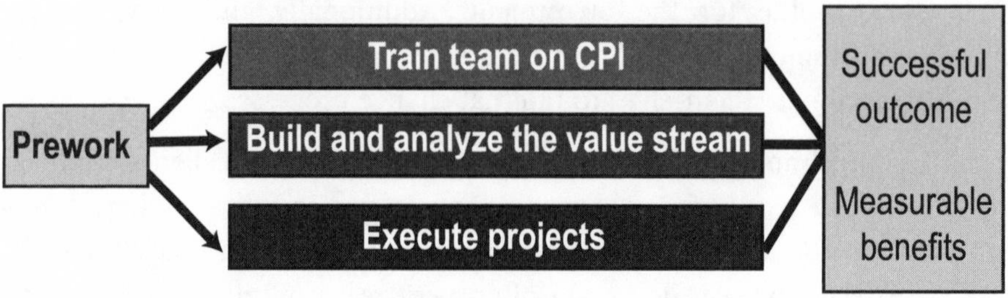

- In the pre-work assessment, the organization's mission and key outcome metrics are identified. Methods like those described in Chapters 2 and 3 can be used to identify high-priority targets. These opportunities are then either refined into individual projects or grouped into a series of linked initiatives. The needs of the organization will determine the best balance of training to build capability and project execution effort.

- After the workshop, participants will continue to "work the plan" and act on identified activities to achieve the project results. Jumping right in gives the knowledge that participants gained immediate relevance. The coaching from experts during this phase gives students the confidence to apply their skills beyond the initial Kaizen event conducted during the training. Before re-assessing the next round of projects, an evaluation of project results should be conducted to ensure that results are being delivered.

Figure 34 shows how the Rapid Path to Results approach generates impact so quickly. One cycle can be completed in as little as 12 weeks, including a 2-week front-end assessment and a 10-week period for execution and capability transfer.

**Figure 34: Model for a 12-Week
Rapid-Path-to-Results Initiative**

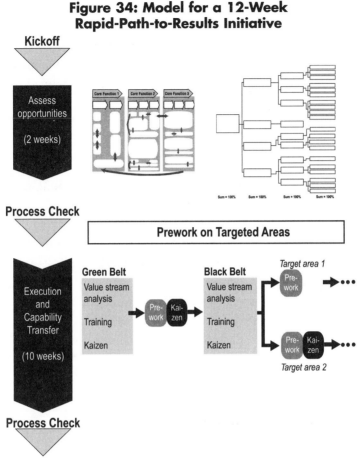

This is a **scalable** model that can deliver results, whether your plan is to conduct a one-day assessment and a five-day workshop on a targeted process metric or a more robust assessment followed by a multi-generational series of workshops linked to broader mission-critical outcomes.

Within each workshop, students apply their training multiple times to internalize the learning and build their skills. This approach utilizes individual or multiple workshops based on the deployment playbook. Students solve real business issues as they apply the appropriate process improvement tools.

As progress is made, the pattern is repeated, resulting in an overall deployment path that is high-performing and low-risk and combines incremental investments with immediate returns.

We've seen more and more organizations adopting this kind of Rapid Path because of its many advantages: it ensures that improvement projects are aligned with strategic objectives, engages the organization to help affect a positive change in culture, and creates end-to-end accountability to drive sustained results and continual improvement toward a defined future end state.

Speed with Results

For much of the past two decades, organizations undertaking an improvement journey had to trust that results would accrue *eventually* but that they would not see anything significant for maybe a year or two. That is no longer the case. As the options presented in this chapter show, there are new pathways that can be adapted to generate the kinds of results your organization needs within a time frame that meets your business needs. You no longer need to sacrifice speed if you want meaningful results, nor do you need to sacrifice results if you want to build capability. Both outcomes can be yours by striking the right balance.

Notes

[1] For more about Public Service Value, see Martin Cole and Greg Parston, *Unlocking Public Value: A New Model for Achieving High Performance in Public Service Organizations* (Hoboken, NJ: John Wiley & Sons, 2006).

[2] *A Proof of the Queueing Formula L=λW* Operations Research, 9, 383-387. John D. C. Little is a professor at MIT. For those trained in statistics, one of the reasons this seemingly obvious equation becomes a law is that it is *distribution independent*; that is, if material arrives in an exponential distribution and departs in a Gaussian distribution, Little's Law still is valid.

[3] For more on Little's Law, see Michael L. George, *Lean Six Sigma for Service: How to Use Lean Speed & Six Sigma Quality to Improve Services and Transactions* (New York, NY: McGraw-Hill, 2003).

[4] For a complete discussion of the concept of value in the public sector, see Martin Cole and Greg Parston, *Unlocking Public Value* (Hoboken, NJ: John Wiley & Sons, 2006).

[5] See also Michael L. George, James Works, Kimberly Watson-Hemphil, *Fast Innovation: Achieving Superior Differentiation, Speed to Market, and Increased Profitability* (New York, NY; McGraw-Hill, 2005).

[6] These three areas were adapted for application to the public sector from the work of Scott D. Anthony, Mark W. Johnson, and Joseph V. Sinfield, "Institutionalizing Innovation," *MIT Sloan Management Review* 49:2, Winter 2008, 45–53. The co-authors are consulting colleagues of Harvard Business School professor Clayton M. Christensen, the originator of the disruptive innovation concept.

[7] Based on the work of Ram Charan, Stephen Drotter, and James Noel, *The Leadership Pipeline: How to Build the Leadership Powered Company* (San Francisco: Jossey-Bass, 2001).

[8] Richard A. Hagberg and Yaarit Silverstone, *Demystifying Leadership: Learning from the Best Leaders* (Chicago: Accenture High Performance Research, March 2009).

[9] U.S. General Accounting Office, *Disaster Response: Criteria for Developing and Validating Effective Response Plans* (September 2010), http://www.gao.gov/new.items/d10969t.pdf. Accessed February 5, 2011.

[10] Sue Bushell, "Chasing Agility," *CIO Magazine* (May 15, 2008), http://www.cio.com.au/article/216333/chasing_agility/. Accessed February 5, 2011.

[11] Global Business Network, *What If: The Art of Scenario Planning for Nonprofits* (2001), http://www.gbn.com/consulting/article_details.php?id=27. Accessed February 5, 2011.

Index

About Us

Though three names appear as authors of this book, the understanding of complex issues and the insights represented here draw not only from their individual experiences but also the work of Accenture Management Consulting and the Accenture Institute for Health & Public Service Value.

ABOUT THE Authors

Mark Price is a senior executive for Accenture Management Consulting and coauthor of the bestselling *The Lean Six Sigma Pocket Toolbook*. He has more than 15 years of consulting experience and has mentored and facilitated executive teams to lead large Lean Six Sigma deployments in both commercial and federal government sectors such as the U.S. Postal Service, U.S. Department of Treasury, U.S. Army, Naval Air Systems Command, ITT Industries, and Alcan.

Walt Mores is a senior executive for Accenture Management Consulting, supporting Health & Public Service clients. Walt started his professional career as a U.S. Naval Officer and Aviator, and has since guided deployments of Lean Six Sigma and other operational improvement methodologies for both commercial and public service clients such as Xerox, Alcan, and, the U.S. Army.

Hundley M. Elliotte is a senior executive and leads the Process Performance Global Offering Group within Accenture Management Consulting. He has more than a decade of consulting experience, and has built value through many client engagements and development of new offerings. Recently, he led the development and implementation of the production ramp-up of mine-resistant (MRAP) vehicles for the U.S. military—the largest weapons ramp-up since WWII.

continued

ABOUT **Accenture Management Consulting**

Drawing on the extensive experience of its 13,000 management consultants globally, Accenture Management Consulting helps clients move from issue to outcome with pace, certainty, and strategic agility. We enable companies and governments to achieve high performance by combining broad and deep industry and functional offerings and capabilities across seven service lines: strategy, customer relationship management, finance & performance management, process & innovation performance, risk management, talent & organization performance, and supply chain management.

Accenture Management Consulting specializes in working with organizations that are facing a broad range of strategic and operational challenges, such as geographic talent shifts, rapidly evolving customer segments and preferences, game-changing technologies, and mounting pressure to improve results.

We help these organizations identify and unlock ***differentiating, sustainable value***. That value could be measured in terms of mission delivery (numbers of clients served, variety of services or produts offered), economic outcomes (stronger growth, greater efficiency and higher capital returns), or operational effectiveness (such as stronger relations with suppliers, better management of scarce resources, unsurpassed operational excellence, or faster innovation cycles).

Accenture is a global management consulting, technology services and outsourcing company. Combining unparalleled experience, comprehensive-capabilities across all industries and business functions, and extensive research on the world's most successful companies, Accenture collaborates with clients to help them become high-performance businesses and governments. Accenture is a leading provider of management consulting services worldwide.

www.accenture.com/federal

About the Accenture Institute for Health & Public Service Value

The Accenture Institute for Health & Public Service Value is dedicated to promoting high performance in the health care sector and in public service delivery, policy-making, and governance. Through research and development initiatives, the Institute aims to help health care and public service organizations deliver better social, economic, and health outcomes for the people they serve.

The Institute undertakes and commissions relevant research; produces publications on good practice in public service; develops practical methods of applying the concepts of public value; and presents events to bring together and promote discussion among public managers and stakeholders in the government, academic, nonprofit, and private sectors.

The Institute has studied dozens of public service organizations around the world to identify the strategic and operational principles for creating public value. In doing so, we have built upon Accenture's long-standing research into high-performance businesses to understand what public service organizations need to do, how they should be organized, and what behaviors they can adopt to help transform into high-performance government organizations.

www.accenture.com/IHPSV